D0276518

Rock and Gem Polishing

a complete guide to amateur lapidary

Rock and Gem Polishing

a complete guide to amateur lapidary

by

Edward Fletcher

London

Blandford Press

First published in 1973

by Blandford Press Ltd,
167 High Holborn, London WC1V 6PH

© 1973 Edward Fletcher

ISBN 0 7137 0617 1

All rights reserved. No part of this book may be reproduced or transmitted in any form or by any means, electronic or mechanical, including photocopying, recording or by any information storage and retrieval system, without permission in writing from the Publisher.

Text set in 12 on 13 Bembo and
printed in Great Britain by
Unwin Brothers Limited,
Old Woking, Surrey
A member of the Staples Printing Group

List of Contents

*To Edwina Bewkey, for her magic in transforming rough
and ready manuscripts into readable books.*

Acknowledgements

The author and publishers are grateful to the following who have
supplied some of the photographs which illustrate this book:

M. L. Beach (Products) Ltd, Figs. 34, 46
Kernowcraft Ltd, Figs. 11, 35, Plate 6
Ammonite Ltd, Figs. 60, 62
Gemrocks Ltd, Figs. 28, 50
Minerals & Gemstones (Penzance) Ltd, Figs. 10, 16, 24
PMR Lapidary Equipment, Figs. 9, 25
A. & D. Hughes Ltd, Fig. 6
E. P. Joseph Ltd, Figs. 22, 23

The remaining black and white photographs and all the colour plates,
except Plate 6, were taken by Michael Allman, F.I.I.P., F.R.P.S.

Thanks are also due to Gemrocks Ltd for their help in supplying stones
and equipment for some of the illustrations, and to John Wood who
drew the line illustrations and the location maps.

Since the publication of my book, *Pebble Polishing*, the hobby of amateur lapidary has grown in popularity by leaps and bounds. Thousands of people who once believed that success at any hobby connected with handicrafts required an artistic flair which only gifted souls possessed have been delighted to discover just how wrong they were. Having bought tumble-polishing machines, and followed half a dozen basic rules, they have produced beautiful hand-made jewellery and proved to themselves that 'artistic flair' is a gift possessed by every one of us and which lies dormant until we provide it with the opportunity to flourish. Now, those same people are asking, 'Where do we go from here?'

I am delighted to report that the further steps in amateur lapidary and home jewellery-making which you are about to take by reading this book are as easy to follow, and equally rewarding, as were those which led to success at tumble-polishing. The equipment—diamond saws, drills, grinding wheels and faceting machines—is as easy and as safe to operate, and will give even more satisfying results. The range of jewellery fittings you will be able to use with the stones you cut and shape is much wider, while the variety of jewellery items you can make is limited only by your own inventiveness.

In *Pebble Polishing* we were concerned with the task of achieving a perfect polish on the outer surfaces of irregularly shaped pebbles and stones which were then attached to simple fittings, such as bell caps, with epoxy resins. In this present book we will examine the various methods of pre-forming rocks and pebbles before putting them into a tumbler, of drilling holes, of slicing pebbles and stones into two equal halves, of polishing large slabs of semi-precious rock to make delightful specimens for a display cabinet, of forming domed cabochons and of cutting steps or facets on transparent and translucent stones.

Readers of *Pebble Polishing* who found the collecting of specimens more exciting than making the jewellery need not despair. The outdoor pleasures of amateur lapidary do not end when one progresses from humble beach pebbles to the more exotic semi-precious gems. It is true that much of the high-quality gem material used in these more advanced techniques comes from foreign lands and is purchased by amateur lapidaries at their local rock shop. Nevertheless, many of the humble beach pebbles described in the earlier book are quite suitable for use with some of the machines we are going to look at. Indeed, there are locations throughout the British Isles where exciting semi-precious gems and minerals can be found by the determined hunter who wishes to cut and polish his own material. Tracking them down is as exciting and as rewarding as searching for amber or cornelians on pebble beaches, and because many are to be found in the wild and remoter parts of Britain, scenic beauty is guaranteed whether or not you succeed in the hunt. Gold, garnets, opal, freshwater pearls, cairngorm, fluorite, amethyst and many other delightful specimens can be found, and detailed knowledge of geology is quite unnecessary in order to track them down. The few basic rules required to locate likely rock formations are given in this book. If you can add to them a certain amount of patience, some careful observation and a little luck, they are as likely to guide you to a valuable gem crystal as is any academic reference book. The collecting maps which I included in *Pebble Polishing* proved so popular with many readers that I have included in this book similar maps to indicate hunting grounds for British gems. They are by no means exhaustive, but will, I hope, lead you to some worthwhile finds.

This book is not a detailed course of instruction in the techniques of advanced lapidary. There are already many books written by experts for experts on the subject, and readers who prefer a more scholarly approach are recommended to look in the reference department of any good bookshop. I have written this book for absolute beginners and for those men, women and children who have tried and succeeded at tumble-polishing and who now wish to take their interest in the hobby a few steps further. It describes in the simplest possible way how to make a start on grinding, drilling, slabbing, faceting and cabochon-cutting. Throughout the book I have concentrated on the least expensive and the simplest machines available at the time of writing, and I have given as many manufacturers as possible an opportunity to provide illustrations and operating instructions for their particular machines. I have also included descriptions and photographs taken during visits to some of the numerous rock shops and lapidary clubs which are now to be found in most towns and cities; and I thoroughly recommend that all readers visit as many shops and clubs as they possibly can. The enthusiasts who run them are mines of information who will be more than pleased to give you the benefit of their experience and knowledge when you decide to buy your equipment or have a question which this book does not answer. Without the help some of those men and women gave me with this present volume, it would probably have remained unwritten.

Finally, a brief word to overseas readers. Lapidary as a hobby is immensely popular in countries such as the United States, Canada and Australia. A number of the machines described in this book are manufactured in those countries and readers living there will have no difficulty in finding a rock shop selling these and many other excellent machines. As for the outdoor aspects of the hobby, I can only say how much I envy you in the wide choice of gem-hunting locations you will be able to visit. The geology in the chapter on gem collecting applies no matter where in the world you live; if you follow the advice given there, your finds should be as exciting as the places you will visit.

1 Cutting a pebble in half

If you have spent a few weekends combing shingle beaches for attractive pebbles you will know how difficult it can be to find matched pairs to make earrings, cufflinks and other items of jewellery which require two stones of similar size, shape and colour. It is a problem which tumble-polishing enthusiasts can only hope to solve by good fortune and patience; and it will come as no surprise, if you have owned a tumbler, to learn that the first task newcomers to more advanced equipment wish to attempt is that of cutting pebbles and small rock fragments into two equal halves. It solves the problem of finding matched pairs at a stroke. Simply select your most attractive finds, cut them in half before loading your tumbler barrel, and you need never again experience the frustration of finding partners for those rare beauties which have a habit of turning up in ones.

The most popular machine for this task is the *trim saw*. It consists of a circular diamond saw blade which is connected to an electric motor by means of two pulleys and a drive belt. The blade is housed in a covered, leak-proof tank which holds sufficient coolant to allow the rim of the blade to be continuously immersed in the liquid as it turns. The top of the tank forms a flat work-table through which the part of the blade which does the cutting protrudes. Behind this protruding part of the blade is a splash guard. This ensures that the spray of coolant which the blade generates as it turns is directed back on to the blade and returns to the tank. A small shield is usually fitted at the front of the machine to protect the operator from splashes.

Fig. I Typical diamond saw layout

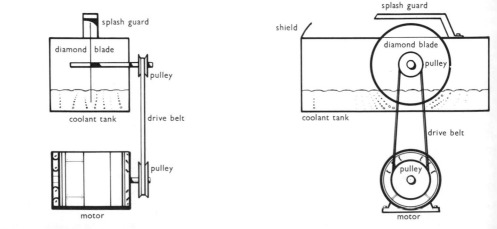

This basic set-up of a motor-driven circular blade partly immersed in a tank of coolant is common to many lapidary saws, and it will be helpful to take a closer look at the various components before we go on to discuss the use of the trim saw.

Diamond blades

Your tumble-polishing experiences will, no doubt, have given you a healthy respect for the hardness of pebbles and semi-precious stones. You will know that it takes many days of continuous rotation inside a barrel to wear away surface cracks and blemishes on tough pebbles, or to grind down the rough edges on crushed rock fragments. How then, you might ask, is it possible to cut a fair-sized beach pebble into two halves in a matter of minutes? The answer is a diamond blade.

Knoop scale

The silicon carbide grits used in the grinding stages of tumble-polishing are extremely hard. On Moh's Scale—the table so often quoted when referring to the relative hardnesses of different gemstones—silicon carbide stands at approximately 9·5. Most of the pebbles and semi-precious stones used in amateur lapidary have a hardness of about 7 on the table and their surfaces can, therefore, be worn down by the abrasive action of silicon carbide which is much harder. Diamond stands at the top of Moh's Scale with a hardness of 10 and it is many, many times harder than silicon carbide, in spite of its proximity on Moh's Scale.

There is another, lesser known table which indicates *comparative* degrees of hardness—unlike Moh's Scale which indicates only *relative* hardnesses—and which shows in a more dramatic way the incredible abrasive power of diamond. On this table, known as the *Knoop Scale*, the average beach pebble stands at 700, silicon carbide stands at about 2,000, while diamond tops the scale at over 6,000, the hardest material known to man.

	Moh's Scale of relative hardness	Knoop Scale of comparative hardness
Calcite	3	135
Fluorite	4	163
Apatite	5	360

Feldspar	6	560
Quartz	7	700
Topaz	8	1,250
Silicon carbide	9.5	2,000
Diamond	10	6,200

Even more remarkable to newcomers to advanced lapidary machines is the fact that diamond blades are absolutely safe to use. Unlike circular saws used in woodwork, lapidary saws hold no dangers for inexperienced fingers. Diamond blades do not have 'teeth' as ordinary sawblades have. Look at one closely and you will see that it is quite smooth on its outer rim, not unlike a gramophone record. The rim is fractionally wider than the remainder of the blade, and it is here that the diamonds which do the cutting are to be found. You cannot see them because they are microscopic in size and consist of tiny fragments of larger diamonds which have been crushed to fine dust, or of man-made diamonds which have been produced by subjecting carbon to tremendous heat and pressure. In the manufacture of some blades, known as *notched rims*, the diamonds are first mixed with metallic powders and inserted into notches cut into the edge of the

Fig. 2 Even when the diamond blade is spinning round, it will not cut your fingers

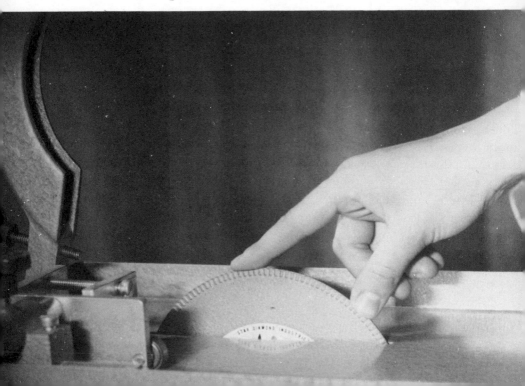

8" X .032

8" X .032

STAR-M

Fig. 3   A diamond sawblade

metal disc. The blade is then heated to a very high temperature so that the diamonds and the metallic powders become fused in the rim. Other blades, known as *sintered rims*, are manufactured by first making thin hoops of fused diamonds and metallic powders which are then soldered on to metal discs to produce the finished blade.

Trim saws are usually fitted with 6 in. or 8 in. diameter blades and, when you buy your machine, the supplier will provide a comprehensive instruction leaflet dealing with the care and use of the blade. These instructions have been written by the blade manufacturer and it is most important that you read them *and* carry them out. An expensive blade can be ruined by failure to do so.

One point which you must be absolutely certain about is whether your blade has been designed to run in one direction only, or is of the type which must be reversed at some time during its working life. Some manufacturers state that their blades must be removed from machines after approximately $\frac{1}{16}$ in. rim wear and reversed so that they cut in the opposite direction to ensure even wear on both sides of the rim. Other manufacturers firmly state that their blades must never be reversed. Hence the need for a very careful reading of instructions supplied with your blade.

Pulleys, motors and drive belts

Some trim saws are supplied without pulleys, motors or drive belts which must be purchased as separate items. It is important that the pulleys fitted to the blade shaft and motor are of the correct size to provide the speed of revolution recommended for the diamond blade. If the trim saw you buy is not fitted with these items, your supplier will tell you the sizes required and will probably stock those which fit your machine.

For the benefit of those few readers who are obliged to work out correct pulley sizes for themselves, let me say that it is a simple calculation. You will find your motor's speed of revolution (r.p.m.) recorded on the small plate attached to the motor casing. It will probably be 1,425 r.p.m. if you are using an ex-refrigerator motor. If the instructions provided with your machine state that the blade speed must be 2,850 r.p.m. and you find a 2-in. pulley connected to the blade shaft, you will require a 4-in. pulley on the motor. This will then drive the blade shaft at twice the motor speed—2,850 r.p.m. In other words, because the pulley on the blade shaft has a diameter half that of the pulley on the motor, it will rotate twice as fast. If you have any difficulty with this calculation, consult a friend with engineering experience or contact a member of your local lapidary club.

Fig. 4   Typical pulley and drive belt arrangement

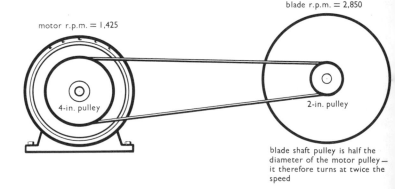

blade r.p.m. = 2,850

motor r.p.m. = 1,425

4-in. pulley

2-in. pulley

blade shaft pulley is half the diameter of the motor pulley— it therefore turns at twice the speed

Many newcomers are perplexed by the fact that the majority of lapidary machines are sold without motors; they are even more perplexed to read in suppliers' catalogues that second-hand refrigerator and washing-machine motors are recommended as ideal for fitting to new saws, grinders and lapping units. The reason why most suppliers prefer to sell machines without motors is simply that if a motor is fitted before despatch to the customer, the weight of the shipping container becomes extremely high. Often it is too high for the container to be sent by mail, and so high that despatch by rail or road proves very expensive. It is fortunately the case that motors fitted to refrigerators, washing machines and spin dryers are ideal for lapidary equipment, and it is also the case that second-hand motors from these appliances can be purchased, for about one-third of the cost of a new motor, at any electrical repair workshop. Furthermore, they can be counted on to give many years of useful life.

Such a motor will usually be what is known as a $\frac{1}{4}$ h.p., continuously rated induction type. This means that it is designed for prolonged running without overheating, that it consumes very little current, that it does not cause radio or television interference and that it will run with the minimum of noise and vibration. Nor does it require much attention during its working life: an occasional light oiling of its bearings, or a spot of grease now and again if it is fitted with grease cups, and long life and hard-working service are assured.

You can, of course, have a motor, pulleys and a drive

Fig. 5 An ex-refrigerator motor is ideal for running a lapidary machine—$\frac{1}{4}$ h.p., induction motor, 240 volts A.C., 50 cycles, 1,425 r.p.m., continuously rated.

drive shaft to which pulley is attached

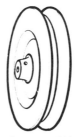

pulleys are available in a wide range of sizes

belt fitted to any machine before you buy; but you must expect to pay additional carriage charges. Alternatively, you can buy your machine from a supplier who sells every machine complete and ready to run. Whether you buy a complete machine or fit your own driving attachments, you should always ensure that the drive belt and pulleys are fitted with safety guards, particularly if the machine is to be used by children. The diamond blade is quite safe, but exposed belts and pulleys can be extremely dangerous to small fingers.

Tanks and coolants

The tank which holds the liquid coolant is one of the most important parts of any lapidary sawing machine, and it must be absolutely leak-proof. If you cut a pebble or a piece of rock with the tank empty or the coolant level too low the diamond blade will be severely damaged and the stone you are cutting will probably fracture. The liquid coolant must be periodically renewed when it becomes contaminated with rock particles, and the tank must, therefore, be easy to clean. This is usually accomplished by fitting a drain plug, and by ensuring that the cutting table which covers the tank can be quickly removed so that the inside walls may be wiped clean.

The coolant in the tank should always be that recommended by the diamond blade manufacturer. Some makers specify light machine oil, others state that a mixture of oil and paraffin should be used, while some recommend a water-soluble coolant which has to be diluted before use. Whatever the coolant, it performs three vital functions. It keeps the diamond blade cool; it cleans the cut by washing out rock fragments as the blade bites into the stone; and it reduces the heat generated in the stone during cutting. In trim saws the level of the coolant in the tank should be such that approximately $\frac{1}{2}$ in. of the blade's rim is immersed at all times. Too little coolant will reduce cutting efficiency; too much is wasteful. The job of cleaning out the sludge which collects in the bottom of the tank is a task which is often neglected because the sludge cannot be seen unless the cutting table is removed. If you bear in mind the important tasks carried out by the coolant, it will help you remember the importance of this chore.

When choosing a trim saw you should look for a model with an uncluttered cutting table which provides adequate space for you to hold your pebble or stone in *both* hands as you present it to the edge of the blade. The table should also have drain holes drilled through it so that any coolant which finds its way on to the flat surface can run back into the tank. It should also have raised edges to contain coolant which might otherwise drip from its sides.

Cutting tables and splash guards

The splash guard should be as close to the blade as possible so that sprayed coolant is directed back on to the blade. It should also be hinged so that it can be raised when you are sawing pieces slightly larger than pebble size. A shield at the front of the cutting table is also desirable as it will protect you from any sprayed coolant not trapped by the splash guard.

You should find all of the above design features built into the machines sold by any reputable lapidary supplier. If you shop around before buying—either by visiting rock shops or by requesting mail order catalogues—you should soon find a reasonably priced and well-designed trim saw which, if used with care and commonsense, will give years of trouble free service.

The ideal situation for your trim saw, once you get it home or have it delivered by the supplier, is in a purpose-built workshop where you can enjoy the pleasures of lapidary insulated from all distractions. Alas, this ideal situation is beyond the reach of most of us; a quiet corner of the kitchen or a few square feet of the garden shed or garage are the best we can hope for. Fortunately, amateur lapidary machines do not take up large amounts of space. Some include a mounting for the motor as a built-in feature so that the unit can be set up in an area no larger than the base of the machine. Others can be mounted

Setting up your machine

Fig. 6   A 6-inch trim saw   complete with motor on portable wooden baseboards which can be stored in cupboards when not required. If using such a board, it is most important that the motor is positioned in such a way that the drive belt connecting the motor pulley and the blade shaft pulley is not too tight. A tight belt will cause unnecessary wear on bearings and can also shorten the life of the blade. Aim instead to have the belt just sufficiently tight to turn the blade shaft pulley without slipping. Incidentally, it is a good idea when making the baseboard to cover the bottom with a sheet of foam rubber which will greatly reduce vibration and noise when the machine is in use. Machines supplied complete with motor will have their pulleys fitted to provide correct belt tension. Do not tamper with them.

Three requirements which the spot you select for your machine should have are a nearby power socket, good light in which to work and access to a tap or sink. *The motor must be wired to a three-pin plug with the earth connection made. Do not use a two-pin plug or connect the machine to a light socket.* On machines supplied complete with a motor, an on/off switch will be provided at some convenient point on the equipment, but if attaching your own motor, a switch will have to be fixed between plug and motor. If you doubt your ability to wire the switch correctly, have the job done by a competent electrician. You can dispense with an on/off switch on the machine if the wall socket is

18

of the type which incorporates its own switch, and if the machine can be situated within easy reach. It is, however, unwise to rely on pulling the plug from the socket as a means of stopping the motor.

If possible set up the machine so that light from a window falls across the cutting table from one side, as this will enable you to work at the machine without obscuring your view of the pebble or stone being cut. Good interior lighting, preferably from an angle lamp which can be directed onto the cutting table, is equally suitable.

A kitchen location for your machine will obviously provide ready access to a tap and sink. Water is used in all lapidary work, particularly with grinding wheels (discussed on p. 47) and it is convenient to have a nearby supply. You can, however, manage quite well with empty washing-up liquid bottles and a few plastic bowls if you are working in a shed or garage. If such a spot has a power supply and good lighting you will not find the lack of a sink and tap an insurmountable problem.

Before attempting to cut pebbles with your new trim saw, read the supplier's instructions for setting up the machine once again to make quite sure that you have carried them out to the letter. These last minute checks are most important. Do not allow your enthusiasm to 'have a go' blind you to the dangers of operating the machine incorrectly.

Last minute checks

It is a good idea to embark upon the more advanced techniques of lapidary armed with a notebook in which you can jot down your comments, questions and other points on machines, methods of cutting and grinding, problems encountered when working with different gemstones or anything else worth noting. When next you visit your local rock shop or lapidary club you can take your notebook and obtain expert opinions and advice on anything you have written down. If the answers to your questions and the comments of more experienced enthusiasts are added to your notes you will have your own 'Book of Lapidary' which will prove invaluable as your interest in the hobby grows. The best time to start such a notebook is now. Make a checklist from the manufacturer's instructions and refer to them each time you use the machine. Such a list might read:

1. Ensure coolant level is correct
2. Check sawblade is secure and correctly positioned on shaft
3. Ensure cutting table is free from rock fragments
4. Check splash guard is secure and does not foul blade
5. Ensure drive belt tension is correct
6. Check that safety guards are correctly fitted over drive belt and pulleys
7. Ensure electrical connections on motor and plug are safe

You will quickly memorize your checklist once you have written it down and you will find that running through the points on it becomes automatic each time you use the machine. Bear in mind that saws and instructions differ. Do not copy out the above list into your notebook. Make your own.

Some diamond blade manufacturers specify that their blades must be broken in before they are used on gemstones by first making two or three cuts in an old and discarded silicon carbide wheel. The purpose of this procedure is to wear away a fraction of an inch of metal on the rim of the wheel in order to expose the diamonds. Few beginners have 'old and discarded silicon carbide wheels' lying around, and a substitute material must usually be found. This should be a piece of *soft* building brick. Find a brick with a sandy texture, break it in half, and try scratching its surface with an old file. If sand grains are removed by the file, the brick is suitable for breaking in your diamond blade. Make sure the coolant level is correct when carrying out this operation, and present the brick to the blade with the same care used when cutting semi-precious stones.

Cutting your first pebble With a bowl of clean water containing a few drops of washing-up liquid close at hand, you should now select a

20

suitable pebble from your stocks. For your first attempt at sawing choose a pebble with a symmetrical shape—ideally a slightly flattened sphere about the diameter of a 10p piece. It must be free from cracks or flaws suggesting internal weakness which could lead to the pebble fracturing during the sawing operation, and it should be evenly coloured so that once you have cut it in half you will have a matched pair.

Before attempting to saw this first pebble, you must practice the method of holding pebbles when presenting them to the saw. To do this, hold the pebble lightly between your forefingers and roll it back and forth across the kitchen table with the two fingers acting as an axle. When this motion feels comfortable, bring your second fingers into contact with the pebble in front of your forefingers. The remaining two fingers on both hands should now be bent and pressed firmly on to the table top as you push inwards with equal force against the sides of the pebble with fore and second fingers. You will now have the pebble in a vice-like grip which holds it squarely against the table top. Now bring your thumbs into contact with the pebble behind your forefingers and press firmly downwards. Your thumbs should be only slightly apart—just wide enough for the saw blade to pass between them. Some ladies may find that their thumbnails are too long to allow the thumbs to be placed comfortably in this position, in which case the nails will have to be cut. Look on this drastic action as a small sacrifice made in the interests of Art, and comfort yourself with the knowledge that you will not damage an expensive diamond blade if you hold the pebbles in the manner described. (*See* Fig. 7.)

Practice this correct hold half a dozen times and then switch on your trim saw and allow the blade to spin freely for a few moments to ensure an adequate supply of coolant to the rim. You may find it encouraging to touch the blade with your thumbs at this point if you have any doubts about the safety of working so close to a spinning blade. Hesitation caused by nervousness when actually cutting the pebble could damage the saw.

Fig. 7 The correct method
of holding a pebble when
slicing it on a diamond saw

Hold the pebble firmly and correctly on the cutting table about half an inch from the blade. Sight between your thumbs to ensure that the blade will cut the pebble centrally, and slowly slide your hands forward until contact is made with the spinning blade. Concentrate on holding the pebble squarely on the table and exert pressure *downwards* with your thumbs. Keep your eyes on the blade to ensure that the cut is straight.

It is of the utmost importance that you do not force the pebble on to the blade in an attempt to cut too quickly. It will take from two to four minutes to slice the pebble, and during this time your efforts must be directed towards keeping the cut straight by maintaining firm contact with the cutting table, and towards preventing the pebble riding up the rim of the saw by pressing downwards with your thumbs. Pressure from behind the pebble should be just sufficient to keep the rim of the blade in firm contact with the cut. If sparks begin to fly, or the blade appears to slow down, you are certainly pressing too hard on the rear of the pebble. With the correct amount of pressure applied you should feel firm and regular contact with the blade and just be able to see the slow but sure progress of the cut.

The two commonest mistakes made by beginners when attempting their first cut are first, putting uneven side pressure on the pebble which causes the cut to wander and can lead to a distorted blade, and secondly, parting the thumbs as the blade nears the end of the cut, which causes small flakes of the pebble to chip off as the saw blade breaks through. Make an effort to avoid both mistakes from the outset.

As soon as the cut is completed, both halves of the pebble should be washed in the bowl of soapy water to remove any coolant which has adhered to the stone. Dry the pieces on an old cloth or disposable tissue and then inspect the result. You should have two cleanly cut halves which can now be tumble-polished to produce a matched pair of delightful stones.

After gaining a little experience at cutting symmetrically shaped pebbles you can attempt to cut a small piece of rough rock which you may have bought at your local rock shop or collected on a rock-hounding expedition. The cutting procedure is the same as outlined above, but you must take even greater care when holding the fragment on the saw

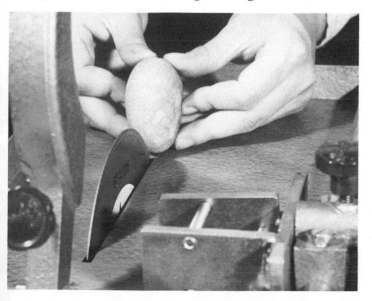

Fig. 8 Slicing the pebble

Fig. 9 Another type of
6-inch trim saw

table and when presenting it to the blade. Always aim to cut a piece of rock in such a way that the largest face is cut first by the blade, and try to have the flattest face against the surface of the table. If you do this, the chances of the blade being deflected as the cut begins will be greatly reduced, and your grip on the stone will be as secure as possible. Two or three hours work with the saw, slicing pebbles and small pieces of rough of different sizes and shapes, should transform you from an absolute beginner to a competent trim-saw operator.

Sharpening the blade

You will be able to slice a very large number of pebbles before your diamond blade needs sharpening, but all blades become blunt when they are repeatedly sawing through hard stone. The first sign of a blunt blade is a much slower cutting action when sawing hard pebbles. This indicates that the diamonds in the rim have become partially covered by metal which has built up around them after being stripped from the rim during cutting. To sharpen the blade, this build-up of metal must be removed in order to expose the diamonds once again. This is done by making two or three cuts in a sandy brick or old silicon carbide wheel. These materials tend to crumble into tiny particles when they are cut, and it is these particles which carry away the build-up of metal on the rim. You *must* have coolant in the tank when making these sharpening cuts which will soon restore the blade's rim to peak condition.

2 Cutting a slab

A slab is a piece of stone taken from a larger mass by making two parallel cuts with the diamond saw blade. It might be a large, thick piece suitable for a book-end or pen stand; or it might be a thin slice which is then cut up into much smaller pieces for jewellery work. Whatever its size, the cutting of a slab involves very similar techniques to those used when slicing a pebble.

The slab saw

The slab saw which does the cutting is also very similar to the trim saws described in Chapter 1. It will probably have a larger blade—anything from 8 in. to 36 in. in diameter—but its basic design will be identical to that of a trim saw. The important difference between the two is that a slab saw is equipped with a vice which holds the stone to be cut by the blade. This is necessary because it would be almost impossible to hold irregularly shaped stones larger than pebble size securely in the hands throughout the cutting action.

You will notice that there is an overlapping of blade sizes in the two types of saw. This has resulted in the production of a hybrid version known as the slab-trim saw which can tackle all of the trim saw's jobs and some of the jobs only carried out on slab saws. A slab-trim saw usually has a blade of 8 in. to 10 in. in diameter, and its vice is removable or hinged at the side of the cutting table so that it can be swung out of the way when trimming work with hand-held stones is carried out. It is, therefore, an extremely useful piece of equipment. If you can afford the slightly

Fig. 10 A versatile slab-trim saw which can be used to cut slabs and trim slices

higher cost of a slab-trim saw fitted with an 8 in. or 10 in. blade I thoroughly recommend it for its advantages over a simple trim saw not equipped with a vice.

Slab saw vices come in a wide range of shapes and sizes, but their basic purpose remains the same no matter how complex their design: that is to hold a piece of rock parallel to the blade so that perfectly straight cuts can be made when slabbing. In its simplest form, the vice consists of two metal jaws which can be screwed together to hold the rock, and which can be made to move along the raised flange or edge of the cutting table parallel to the blade. The jaws are opened and the piece of rock positioned so that it protrudes sufficiently to be cut by the blade. The jaws are then closed again and, with the motor switched on, the vice is pushed along the edge of the table as the rock is fed to the blade. When the cut is completed, the jaws are returned to the front of the table and opened to allow the rock to be moved forward slightly before they are closed and tightened again. A second cut is then made and a parallel-sided slab is thus cut from the rough rock.

The obvious problem with this simple vice is the difficulty experienced in moving the rock forward for the second cut while at the same time keeping the newly cut face parallel to the blade. Less obvious is the problem of side movement which occurs during the cut because the vice is not securely

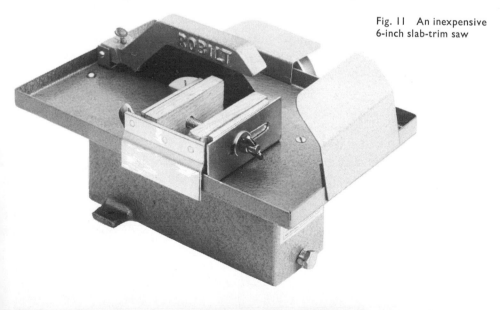

Fig. 11 An inexpensive
6-inch slab-trim saw

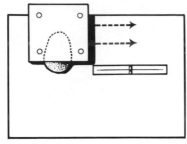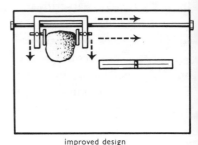

simple vice – jaws fit
loosely over raised
edge of table. After
first cut jaws must
be opened and stone
moved across table

improved design
vice – runs on parallel
bars bolted to ends
of table. Jaws can be
moved across the
table after first cut
without disturbing
the stone

Fig. 12   Slab saw vices   attached to the cutting table. To overcome the difficulty experienced in moving the rock forward for the second cut, more advanced machines are fitted with vices which can be moved *across* the cutting table as well as along it. This means that the second cut can be made without moving the rock in the jaws. Instead the jaws themselves are moved across the table while the rock face remains parallel to the blade.

To prevent the vice moving sideways because it is insecurely fixed to the table, more advanced machines have vices which run along the table on firmly bolted parallel bars. This arrangement ensures that the jaws move smoothly and eliminates the possibility of side movement during the cut.

More sophisticated slab saws have vices which are moved along the cutting table by a weight-feed mechanism which drives the vice at the correct speed for perfect cutting. Others have vices which are moved along their guide bars at the correct cutting speed by a drive connected to the same spindle on which the blade turns, while those with blades of 10 in. or more in diameter are also usually equipped with large plastic covers in addition to the splash guard behind the blade. The cover ensures that the substantial amounts of spray thrown up by large blades are contained within the area of the cutting table. Obviously such machines cost rather more than those equipped with smaller blades and vices which are moved by hand, but they are worth considering if large amounts of slabbing work are planned.

The importance of reading the instructions supplied with your slab saw *before* you attempt to use it cannot be over emphasized. Pour the correct amount of coolant into the tank, check that the diamond blade is secure, ensure that drive belt tension is correct and electrical connections are sound and carry out all other pre-running instructions given. The size of rock you can slab on your saw is limited by the diameter of the blade and by the maximum width between the jaws of the vice. The instructions will tell you the largest recommended size of rock which should be worked on your particular model. *Never, under any circumstances, exceed the recommended limit.* You will almost certainly damage the blade if you do.

Familiarize yourself with the way in which the vice works before you switch on the motor. Try clamping rocks of different sizes and shapes in the jaws, bearing in mind that the jaws must hold the rock even more firmly and securely during the cutting action than you held your pebbles when using the trim saw. The slightest movement of the rock in the jaws during cutting will ruin an expensive blade. The jaws of some vices are faced with softwood or leather to improve their grip on the rock. If your vice has unfaced metal jaws you should cut two pieces of softwood or leather which you can insert between the rock and the metal faces as you tighten them. Remember that the thickness of the material will reduce the size of rock which can be held in the vice.

Once satisfied that you fully understand the workings of the vice, select a piece of rock from which to cut your first slab. It must be free from cracks or flaws which might cause it to fracture during cutting, and it should have as few sharp edges as possible. A squarish or oblong piece would be ideal, but is not always possible to find. Examine the shape of the piece carefully to decide the best possible cutting angle, and bear in mind that flat surfaces are held most securely in the jaws. If your saw has a vice which can

Cutting your first slab

29

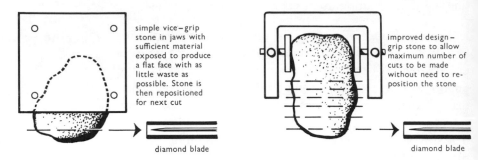

simple vice–grip stone in jaws with sufficient material exposed to produce a flat face with as little waste as possible. Stone is then repositioned for next cut

improved design – grip stone to allow maximum number of cuts to be made without need to re-position the stone

diamond blade

diamond blade

Fig. 13 Holding the stone in the vice

be moved across the saw table you should grip the stone between the jaws in such a way that two or more slabs can be cut without the need to re-position the stone. This will ensure parallel sides on each slab cut. If your vice cannot be moved across the table grip the stone so that the first cut will produce a flat face on the stone with as little waste as possible.

When you are satisfied that the jaws have a really firm hold on the stone and there is no danger of the stone slipping during the cut, start the motor and move the vice along the raised edge or guide bar to within an eighth of an inch of the blade. Check that the splash guard will not foul the stone as the cut proceeds and, if necessary, move it rearwards to provide a free run for the vice. With a firm and steady grip on the rear of the vice, ease the stone on to the rim of the blade. The cut must be completed in a single and continuous movement; pressure from the rear must not be so great that the blade begins to slow or sparks fly from the cut. The rate of feed varies with different materials and is largely dependent on the thickness of the rock being cut, but it is better to err on the side of slowness than to try to force the blade to do too much. As you near the end of the cut, place your fingers lightly on the waste piece which is about to fall, and prevent it from slipping into the blade slot on the table. With this first cut completed, slide the vice rearwards and switch off the motor.

When you look at the newly cut face you are sure to be delighted at the beauty the blade has revealed, and you will

Fig. 14   Cutting a slab

be able to form an idea of what the slab might look like when polished. Run your fingers across the face. It should be fairly smooth and free from deep blade marks which would indicate that the blade, vice or stone had moved sideways during the cut. If all is well you must now decide the thickness of your first slab.

This will depend on how you plan to use the finished piece. Slabs for book-ends, pen stands and other large items will probably be half an inch or more in thickness; slabs which are to be cut into smaller shapes for jewellery-making must be as thin as possible in order to reduce the amount of grinding necessary to form the finished article. Beginners are advised to cut slabs which are intended for jewellery-making a little thicker than more experienced amateur lapidaries might cut them. A slab which is cut slightly thicker than actually required will need more work during the grinding stages, but the surplus material provides an opportunity to correct mistakes made during grinding without spoiling the piece. If, on the other hand, the slab is cut very close to the final dimensions of the finished item, a mistake made during the grinding stages can spell complete ruin for the piece of jewellery. Cut thicker slabs until you have gained experience at grinding.

If your slab saw has a simple vice, you must now solve the problem of moving the stone for the second cut while keeping the face parallel to the diamond blade. One method of doing this is to use an accurately sawn piece of wood which can be held against the opposite side of the cutting table to act as a fence when the stone is loosened in the vice and its sawn face pressed against the wood before the jaws are tightened once again. The wood must be cut to provide the width of slab required, a number of pieces being needed for different slab thickness. If the vice has movable jaws the task is simple: the screws holding the jaws are simply loosened and jaws and stone are pushed across the table to give the required slab thickness. Remember to allow for the thickness of the blade when setting the jaws. Looked at from the vice side of the table it is the *outside* edge of the blade which will determine the thickness of the slab when it is cut.

When the stone has been moved forward and checked for security between the jaws, switch on the motor and proceed with the second cut in exactly the same way as before. Use your fingers as gentle supports as the blade reaches the end of the cut, to prevent the slab from falling, and wash the slab in your bowl of soapy water to remove the smear of coolant left by the blade. If two or more slabs are required, and you have a movable vice, simply adjust the jaws each time you make a cut until you have the number of slabs required or the jaws are fully extended. If you wish to cut slabs of equal thickness, use a wooden guide fence as suggested for use with simple machines each time you move the jaws. This will ensure that the jaws are moved the same distance across the table after each cut.

Fig. 15   Using a wooden guide fence

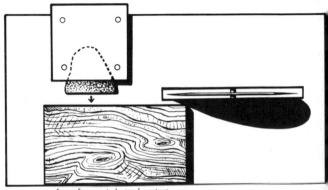

face of stone is butted against
accurately sawn piece of wood
before jaws are tightened for
second cut

Prolonged use of the diamond blade to slab hard materials, such as agate, will dull the cutting edge. Sharpen in the same way as a trim-saw blade, keeping the coolant level correct during the operation. If yours is a blade which must be reversed at certain times during its working life, do not forget this important task.

Blade sharpening and sludge cleaning

You will be able to cut many slabs before it becomes necessary to change the coolant in the tank, but it is wise to develop the habit of checking the amount of sludge build-up regularly. When the coolant becomes so contaminated with rock dust and fragments that it must be changed, proceed as follows. Remove the cutting table and agitate the coolant so that as much of the sludge as possible is washed from the bottom of the tank and held in suspension. Next, take a wide-mouthed glass jar and hold it beneath the drain hole as you unscrew the plug. Allow the contaminated coolant to drain into the jar as you wipe the internal walls of the tank to remove all traces of rock particles. You can now replace the drain plug, tighten it securely, and refill the tank with clean coolant to the required level before replacing the cutting table. Do not throw away the contaminated coolant. Leave the jar undisturbed for a day and the sludge will settle on the bottom. The clean coolant can then be carefully poured off and used again in the tank when next you clean it out. Dispose of the sludge by pouring it into a plastic bag which can then be placed in your dustbin. It should never be poured down drains or sinks.

3 Grinding and polishing a flat surface

Large, flat surfaces, particularly those produced by a slab saw, are usually brought to a final polish on a lapping unit. This piece of equipment is similar in design to a record player and has a flat turntable, or lap as it is known, which is made to revolve by means of an electric motor, pulleys and a drive belt. The lap is made from cast iron and turns at 300 to 500 r.p.m., which is slower than the speed at which your diamond saw works, but much faster than a record player's top speed of 78 r.p.m. The motor is usually similar to that fitted to a diamond saw, the slower speed of revolution being achieved by the use of a larger pulley on the turntable shaft. For example, an 8 in. pulley on the lap shaft and a 2 in. pulley on the motor would produce a working speed of 356 r.p.m.

Cast-iron laps

The cast-iron lap is mounted horizontally inside a bowl or open tank, and loose silicon carbide grits which have been mixed with a little water to produce a light paste are applied to the flat turntable. The motor is switched on and the slab of rock placed face downwards on the spinning lap wheel where it is held in firm contact with the surface

Fig. 16 A well designed lapping unit

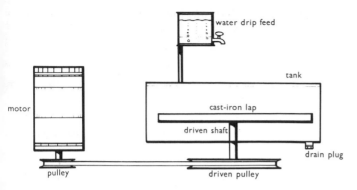

Fig. 17 The layout of a cast-iron lap

throughout the grinding operation. As with tumble-polishing, progressively finer grades of silicon carbide are used on the lap until a perfectly smooth surface is achieved. To polish the slab, the cast-iron lap is replaced by another faced with felt or leather which is sprinkled with cerium oxide and a little water. A few minutes work with this will soon produce a mirror finish on the smooth slab.

Cast-iron laps range from 6 in. to 18 in. in diameter and you should consider the size of slab you wish to grind and polish when choosing a machine. If your budget limits your choice to smaller machines, select one which is fitted with a lap without a centre hole or protruding nut as this will mean that the entire area of the lap can be used without damaging the stone. Such laps have threaded bolts on their undersides which screw into the driven shaft.

Another design feature to look for when buying a machine is ease of cleaning. No matter how carefully you apply the silicon carbide to the lap, a certain amount will be thrown off as the wheel spins. This means that the surfaces of the bowl or tank must be cleaned regularly. Some laps are fitted with a drain plug and a waste pipe which can be fed into a bucket placed on the floor near the machine; while others are so designed that water and grits which fly from the lap collect at the front of the container where they can be easily wiped from the surface. Fairly high sides on the rim of the lap bowl are also necessary to catch the drops of silicon carbide paste thrown from the revolving turntable.

35

As with other lapidary machines, these units are sold with and without motors, pulleys and drive belts, and it is important when buying a machine without these components to ensure that pulleys of the correct size are fitted, in order to achieve the speed of revolution recommended by the manufacturer. A lap which spins too quickly will throw off all the silicon carbide paste; a lap running slowly will take much too long to grind the surface of the slab to a smooth finish.

Some units are fitted with a water reservoir which is mounted above the lap and which incorporates a tap and plastic pipe so that water can be directed on to the lap either as a drip feed during the grinding process, or as a continuous flow to clean the lap between different grinding stages. On other machines, an empty squeezy bottle must be used in place of the water reservoir.

Also available are a number of sophisticated and more expensive units known as vibrating laps which have special bearings and drive shafts enabling them to vibrate in such a way that any slab placed upon their surfaces is moved automatically throughout the process without the need to hold the stone in the hand. Like the conventional lapping units dealt with here, they also use silicon carbide grits for grinding and cerium oxide as a polishing agent; but it is essential when using a vibrating lap that the manufacturer's instructions on grades of silicon carbide to be used and on methods of operation are strictly followed. Ordinary lapping machines offer more scope for experiments with grits, polishes and grinding times.

It is worth mentioning that many rock shops sell a wide range of pre-slabbed stone. If you cannot afford a slab saw *and* a lapping unit, but wish to polish flat slabs, you can get along quite well without the saw if you buy ready-sawn slabs which you can then polish on your own lapping machine. The excitement of cutting a rough rock on a saw in order to reveal its hidden beauty will be missed, but you will be able to select the best slabbed material offered by your supplier to produce your finished specimens and make your jewellery.

Once you have set up the machine in accordance with the **Other equipment**
manufacturer's instructions, there are a number of other
items you must have in order to produce perfectly polished
flat surfaces. The first on the list is a supply of ready-cut
slabs. Often, when a slab is sawn, the piece breaks from the
parent rock a moment before the diamond blade reaches
the end of the cut. This leaves a slight projection, or nib,
on the edge of the slab which must be removed before it
can be placed flat upon the cast-iron lap. Ideally this nib
should be ground flat on a coarse grinding wheel, and if
you have a grinder it is also wise to grind a very slight bevel
around the entire edge of each slab before lapping commences. This will ensure that an absolutely flat surface is
presented to the lap each time a slab is worked. If you do
not have a grinder, the nib can be successfully tackled with
a stout pair of pliers. Grip it between the jaws and give a
sharp twist, or hit the head of the pliers smartly with a
hammer, and the nib should break off cleanly. You will
not be able to grind a bevel on each of your slabs, but if
they are presented to the lap carefully this should not
present too great a problem.

When buying slabbed stone you should always examine
the pieces carefully for cracks, deep imperfections or saw
blade marks and reject any piece which is obviously going
to break or require a large amount of lapping before it is
smooth. You should also reject any piece which has not
been cut with absolutely parallel sides. No amount of work
on the lapping machine will put matters right if the slab
has been incorrectly cut on the saw.

The next item required is a supply of loose silicon carbide
in a number of grades from coarse to very fine, together
with a polishing powder. As explained in my earlier book,
Pebble Polishing, silicon carbide is graded by being passed
through a series of fine mesh screens. The coarse No. 80
grit gets its name from the fact that it has passed through a
screen with 80 meshes to the inch; the higher the grade
number, the finer the individual grains. The range of grits
available runs from 80 to over 1,000 but you will not need
many grades in order to grind your slabs smooth. The best

37

general purpose grades for work on cast-iron laps are Nos. 80, 220 and 400. Cerium oxide is the most widely used polishing agent in all branches of amateur lapidary and it is recommended for slab-polishing on horizontal laps.

The importance of avoiding contamination when working with loose silicon carbide and cerium oxide cannot be over-emphasised. A single grain of No. 80 grit which finds its way into a container holding 400 grit or cerium oxide renders both quite useless for grinding and polishing work. Cleanliness and careful storage will avoid this disaster. Keep your materials in marked containers with secure lids, and check carefully that any spoon or other instrument used when measuring quantities is scrupulously clean.

Finally, you will need a supply of water, a number of plastic containers and a method of applying pastes of grit and water to the lap turntable. If your unit has a water reservoir this should be filled before work commences. Otherwise fill one or two empty washing-up liquid bottles with water and stand them close to the machine. The grits and water can be mixed to light pastes in small plastic bowls and placed nearby ready for application to the lap with a small spoon. Some enthusiasts suggest a paint brush for this last task but, unless a separate brush is used for each grade of silicon carbide, there is a danger that odd particles of coarse grit will be held in the bristles of the brush no matter how thoroughly they are washed. I have seen those small spray bottles on sale at most chemists' shops used very successfully for applying the pastes to the lap but, again, a separate bottle should be used for each grade.

Using the lap   Small amounts of each grade of silicon carbide to be used should be mixed with water to form light pastes. Bear in mind the importance of avoiding contamination, and do not mix too much at once. The correct amount depends on the size of your slab and on how cleanly the surface has been cut with the diamond blade. It is better to mix too little than to overdo things and waste expensive grit. More can always be mixed very quickly if needed. Start with a small tea-spoonful of each and experiment with quantities as your

38

experience grows. Do not add too much water when making up the pastes. Additional water can be dripped onto the lap during grinding if you have underestimated; whereas a paste which is too watery to begin with will fly from the lap before grinding commences.

With the motor switched on, a small amount of coarse paste should be applied to the centre of the lap from where it will quickly spread across the surface. Hold the slab firmly by its edges and present the face to the spinning lap in such a way that the front edge, or toe, of the piece, which will be furthest from your wrist, makes contact with the turntable first. The heel is then pressed down gradually until the slab is absolutely flat on the lap. You must *always* place the slab on the turntable *in the direction of rotation* otherwise the slab will be jerked violently from your hand by the spinning lap. It is rather like stepping on to a moving staircase: a flowing action must be developed if a smooth start is to be made.

No hard and fast rules about grinding times can possibly be given; each slab must be treated as an individual grinding and polishing task with each step in the process lasting as long as is necessary. The aim of the first grind, in which No. 80 grit will be used unless otherwise stated by the lap manufacturer, is to remove from the surface of the slab *all* marks left by the cutting action of the diamond blade. This might take as few as three or four minutes if the cut was accurate and the stone relatively soft and free from cracks

Fig. 18   Placing a slab on the lap.

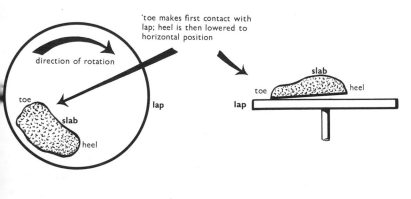

Fig. 19 Holding a slab on a
flat lap

and other imperfections, or it might take anything up to
half an hour. The key to success lies in having the patience
to continue lapping until *all* marks from the previous
operation are removed.

The slab must not be allowed to remain motionless on
the lap, but should be moved across the surface in a circular
or figure-of-eight motion. It must also be turned in the
hand as grinding is carried out. This continuous movement
is necessary because the outer edges of the circular lap move
at a greater speed than the area around the centre. To avoid
uneven grinding of the slab's surface it must, therefore, be
worked across all parts of the lap.

The amount of pressure which your hand must apply to
the slab depends on the slab's weight and its surface area.
There is no definite rule, and you will have to experiment
with different pressures as you carry out the operation.
Certainly your grip on the stone must be sufficiently positive
to prevent the slab flying from your hand; but pressure
must not be so great that the lap slows down. In practice
you will find that you soon develop a 'feel' for the correct
pressure. The grits sound as though they are grinding the
face when the right amount of downward pressure is
applied. If pressure is insufficient, the slab seems to glide
across the surface of the lap; too much and it tends to drag.

As surface imperfections are removed, the pastes tend to

thicken because dust and fine particles of stone mix with them during the grinding operation. Small amounts of water must, therefore, be dripped on to the lap as it spins so that the pastes remain fluid in consistency. The slab should be removed from the lap every few minutes and inspected so that grinding progress can be gauged. Rinse the face under running water or wash it in one of your bowls and examine it under a good light. Turn the slab through a few degrees as the light falls on the face, and run your finger across the surface to decide whether or not further coarse grinding is required. Remember that the aim of this first stage is to remove all blade marks. If more coarse grinding is required return the slab to the lap, placing the toe down first, and continue to move it across the surface until you are satisfied that all blade marks have been removed.

When this coarse grinding stage is completed, it must be followed by a thorough washing operation to remove every trace of coarse grit from the lap, the slab and your hands. The lap can be washed by turning the water reservoir tap full on and allowing water to fall on the cast-iron turntable as it spins. Alternatively, a jet of water from one of your plastic bottles can be directed across the surface. On machines fitted with a drain plug, this water will flow down the waste pipe and carry the used grit and rock particles to the sludge

Fig. 20 Examining the surface of a slab to check grinding progress

bucket. Other readers may have to empty the bowl by hand.

After carefully washing the slab and your hands, you are ready to carry out the intermediate grinding stage using No. 220 grit. The procedure is exactly as for the coarse grind, but the aim of the operation is different. You are now attempting to remove all marks left on the face by the coarse silicon carbide. Use the same figure-of-eight motion when holding the stone on the lap and examine the surface repeatedly during the operation for any high spots which might develop if pressure on the stone is uneven. Continue this stage until you are satisfied that all marks left by the No. 80 grit have been worn down, and follow this with a careful washing of the lap, the slab and your hands once again. You are now ready for the final grinding stage.

Silicon carbide grits as fine as the No. 400 grade you will use during the next stage have very limited abrasive powers. Their purpose is to impart an absolutely smooth finish to the flat surface of the slab. They will not remove deep scratches from the surface of the stone and you should only proceed to the third stage when you are satisfied that all scratches have been removed by the coarser No. 220 grit. If you start the third stage too soon you will fail to achieve a mirror finish on your slab when you go on to the polishing process. This third stage is carried out in the same way as the previous stages. Even greater care should be taken to ensure that every trace of grit is washed away before the polishing stage commences. At the end of the process your slab should be absolutely flat and absolutely smooth.

Polishing
On some units a second lap is provided for polishing. This might be a metal or wooden disc which has a leather or felt buff fixed to its surface. The cast-iron lap is unscrewed from the shaft and replaced by the polishing lap. On other units the cast-iron lap remains in position and is covered by a felt disc which is held in place by a clip tightened around the outer rim.

With the leather or felt in position water is dripped onto the surface until the disc is uniformly moistened. Cerium

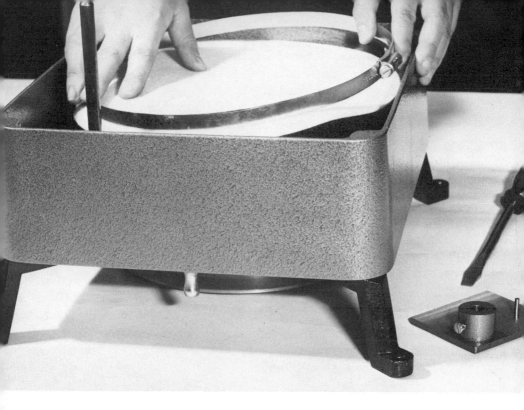

Fig. 21 Fitting a polishing disc to an 8-inch flat lap

oxide powder is then sprinkled on the pad, the motor is switched on, and polishing then commences. With uniform pressure applied to the slab, it is worked across the surface of the polishing buff using the same motion as in the grinding processes. On no account must the pad be allowed to dry out during this stage. Ensure a steady drip feed of water to the buff in order to maintain a creamy cerium oxide and water paste on the surface. More powder may be added to the lap as required.

Greater downward pressure on the slab is usually needed at this stage in order to impart a polish to the face and great care must be taken to ensure that your grip on the slab does not slip. This can happen quite easily if too much of the slippery polishing paste is allowed to build up on the sides of the stone. Rinse the slab in clean water to reduce this build-up and examine the face regularly to check on the finish achieved. As soon as the entire area of the face has been given a mirror finish you should end the polishing stage. Over-polishing tends to dull rather than improve the finish. A final rinse in clean water should reveal a perfectly polished slab.

When grinding and polishing very thin slabs it is difficult to hold the stone firmly as it is pressed on to the lap. This can result in the slab flying from the hand and being damaged on the side of the bowl. To overcome this problem a block of wood can be temporarily attached to the back of the slab using an adhesive which can be removed later with acetone or methylated spirit when the slab is polished.

Using your slabs   Thick slabs which have been polished on both surfaces and symmetrically shaped on a saw make delightful book-ends. If used as flat bases for penholders or table-lamps only the upper face will require polishing. The base can be covered with baize or felt to prevent scratches on desks or tabletops. Thin slabs which have been polished on both surfaces can

Figs. 22 and (*opposite*) 23
Two delightful polished
specimens

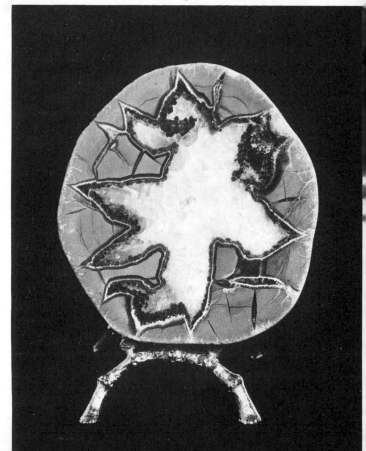

Fig. 23

be cut into small squares on your trim saw and used for a wide variety of jewellery items; while smaller slabs with their edges left in a rough and natural state make very attractive pendants. Beautiful display specimens can also be made by simply cutting large stones into two halves and polishing the faces. In contrast, the remainder of the stone is left in its natural state. Such pieces make ideal doorstops, paperweights and unusual ornaments.

4 Preforming stones before tumbling

Your tumble-polishing machine should not be looked upon as redundant when you progress to more advanced lapidary equipment. Indeed, there is an excellent case for investing in a larger tumbler if you propose to take up the hobby enthusiastically because tumblers are far more versatile when used in conjunction with other lapidary machines. This is clearly seen in the production of preforms which will be discussed in this chapter.

Grinding machines

Preforms are stones which have been cut and roughly shaped *before* they are placed in a tumbler barrel. A sliced pebble is one example, but many more shapes including squares, cubes, ovals, hearts, crosses and triangles can also be made. Those having straight edges can be made using diamond saws only and by carrying out all grinding and polishing in the tumbler barrel; but to produce the widest possible range of preforms you will also need a grinding machine. Since this is also the machine on which cabochons are formed it makes a worthwhile addition to your workshop.

Fig. 24 A large tumbler makes a useful addition to a lapidary workshop

Fig. 25 A robust grinding machine with coarse and fine wheels

In its simplest form a grinder consists of a shaft driven by an electric motor, pulleys, and a drive belt in much the same way as a diamond saw is powered. On the ends of the shaft are fitted coarse and fine silicon carbide grinding wheels usually measuring 6 to 8 in. in diameter and 1 in. in thickness, the most popular grades being Nos. 100 and 220. Because water is an essential requirement when grinding, the wheels are surrounded by splash guards and a shallow tray is placed beneath them in order to catch any water used in the process. A drip feed similar to that used with the lapping unit is usually incorporated in the design, though some machines rely on empty washing-up liquid bottles. A drain plug and waste pipe complete the water circulation system. On most units a rubber strip is attached to the front edge of the splash guard to further reduce the spray of

47

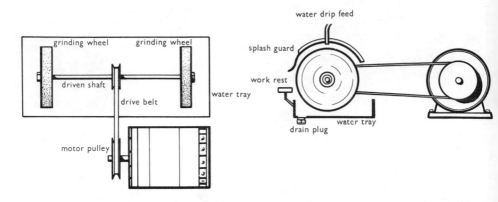

Fig. 26 Basic grinding machine layout

water from the wheels, and some models have a metal work-rest to support the hand during grinding operations.

This basic set-up is quite suitable for shaping preforms prior to tumbling, but other attachments are required in order to produce cabochons which are ground, sanded and polished on the same machine. For the benefit of those readers confused by the terms grinding and sanding let me explain that grinding involves the removal of large amounts of stone in order to bring a particular piece to a regular shape, and sanding refers to the more delicate work of preparing the surface of the stone for its final polish by removing all scratches produced during grinding. A unit designed for grinding, sanding and polishing work usually has its coarse and fine grinding wheels in the centre of the shaft. On one end of the shaft is mounted a sanding disc which consists of a circular piece of wood or metal covered with a hard rubber pad. On to this pad sheets of fine silicon carbide sanding paper are temporarily glued with 'Copydex' or a similar adhesive. The grits on these sheets are graded from Nos. 320 to 600 and because the sheets are attached to a rubber pad they mould themselves to the shape of rounded stones during the sanding operation.

On the other end of the shaft is mounted a hard felt pad which is used during the polishing process in the same way as the horizontal polishing pad is used on a lapping machine. Because the speed at which polishing is carried out is much

48

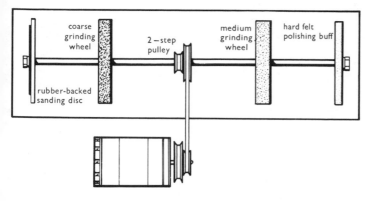

coarse grinding wheel

2-step pulley

medium grinding wheel

hard felt polishing buff

rubber-backed sanding disc

slower than the grinding speed, the shaft and the motor spindles are fitted with two or more pulleys of different sizes so that the speed of revolution can be varied by moving the drive belt. Thus the entire process of grinding, sanding and polishing a stone can be carried out on a single machine. We will return to this three-in-one unit in the next chapter. Meanwhile, let us consider the methods used to produce preforms for tumbling.

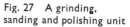

Fig. 27 A grinding, sanding and polishing unit

If you own a slab saw you can start with large pieces of rock and turn out slabs to your own requirements. They should be cut quite thin because the next step is to cut them into smaller pieces on your trim saw. If you do not own a slab saw concentrate on looking for thin, parallel-sided slabs when hunting through stocks at your local rock shop.

To work out the various shapes you wish to produce on the surface of the slab an aluminium pencil is used. This will leave a clear mark on the surface of the slab which can be used as a guideline when sawing. The pencils can be purchased for a few pence at most rock shops. When marking out squares and oblongs the only other tool required is a ruler, but for shapes such as hearts and circles you will need a template. These are also sold at rock shops, and when buying you should select one made in transparent plastic material in preference to one made in metal. The plastic type enables you to see the surface of the slab as you mark out the various shapes and you will be able to move the

49

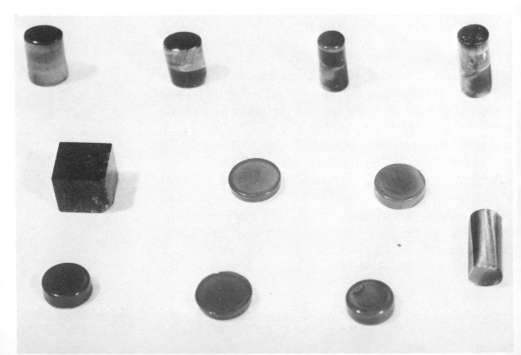

Fig. 28   A combined
grinder, sander, polisher

Fig. 29   Preform shapes
cut with a trim saw from
a larger slab and roughly
shaped on a grinding
wheel before tumbling

template across the slab to select the most attractive patterns in the stone. After marking out the preforms, the slab is cut into smaller pieces on your trim saw. Remember that the diamond blade must only be used to make straight cuts. *You must never attempt to cut curved shapes with a diamond blade.* Continue trimming with straight cuts around the outline until as much waste material as possible has been removed.

The next step is **to** grind away the remaining waste using your coarse silicon carbide grinding wheel. Ensure that the manufacturer's instructions regarding setting up the machine have been carried out, and if your grinder is fitted with two or more pairs of pulleys, move the drive belt to the pair which turn the shaft at the fastest speed. Fill the water reservoir or your plastic bottles and run the waste pipe from the drain plug in the tray to a nearby bucket. *Do not allow water to run onto the grinding wheels when the motor is switched off and the wheels are stationary.* If you do so the wheels could be thrown out of balance because they will absorb too much water on that part of their rims directly beneath the taps. Here is the sequence of operation when grinding:

1. Switch on motor so that wheels are turning
2. Turn on water feed
3. Carry out grinding operations
4. Turn off water feed and allow water to drain from tray
5. Switch off motor to bring wheels to rest

Fig. 30 Marking and cutting preform shapes with a template

template

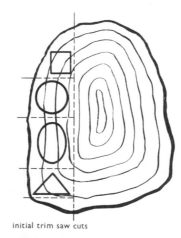

initial trim saw cuts

secondary cuts to remove waste

rough shape ready for grinding

Because the grinding wheels are porous, too much water must never be used. On the other hand, the importance of the small amount of water fed to the grinding surface cannot be over-emphasized. Water is as important in grinding as is coolant when using a diamond blade. It cools the surface of the stone which is being shaped and prevents fractures caused by overheating, it washes away particles of grit and stone which would otherwise clog the surface of the wheel and reduce grinding efficiency, and it prevents dust particles rising into the air by carrying all wastes to the water tray beneath the wheels.

Care of grinding wheels From time to time throughout its life your coarse grinding wheel will require a little maintenance in order to keep its face absolutely flat. Repeated heavy grinding of agate and similar hard materials inevitably results in a number of minor indentations on the face of the wheel. If the stone you are working tends to bounce and bump as you pass it across the wheel it is an indication that the face is not absolutely flat. Putting matters right is known as dressing the wheel, and special diamond-tipped wheel dressers are available which can be passed across the face to re-align it by wearing down the bumps. An equally effective job can be done using a piece of agate slab which has been cut absolutely square. This dressing takes longer but it saves the cost of the diamond tool.

To dress the wheel take the agate slab and present its edge to the spinning wheel at the centre of the rim. Hold the slab firmly and move it gradually towards the wheel until it meets the first of the high spots. Keep the slab square to the wheel and the bump will be worn level with the face. Continue dressing until all imperfections have been removed and remember to use the correct sequence of operation when turning the drip feed on and off. Fine grinding wheels rarely require dressing if used correctly because the really hard grinding work should always be carried out on the coarse wheel. However, should your No. 220 wheel require attention the procedure is exactly the same.

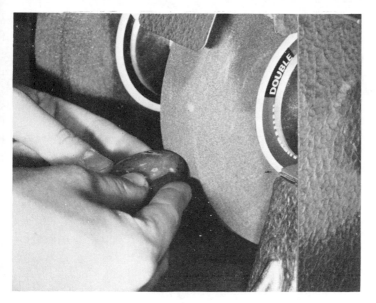

Fig. 31 Presenting the
preform to the grinding
wheel

With the motor running and the drip feed supplying the correct amount of water to the wheel, stand at the front of the machine with the first of your roughly sawn preforms. Grinding is carried out on the rim of the wheel—that is on the 1 in. thickness of its face—the sides being only occasionally used in cabochon forming. The secret of success is to keep the stone constantly moving from side to side across the rim so that the wheel wears evenly. Grooves and pits will quickly develop if you allow the stone to remain in contact with one point for too long.

Hold the preform firmly between fingers and thumb and present it to the wheel with a light, stroking motion back and forth across the face. Preforms should be shaped on the wheel so that their edges are flat. If sloping edges are formed they tend to fracture during the tumble-polishing stage and spoil an otherwise perfect piece. To produce flat edges on your stones make sure that you carry out all coase grinding at the centre of the rim. If the stone is held above or below this centre line the edge will follow the curved shape of the wheel as it is formed.

Square, oblong and triangular shaped preforms should be held firmly in the hand and passed across the wheel with

Grinding your preforms

53

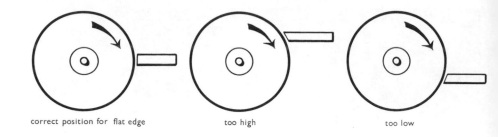

correct position for flat edge   too high   too low

Fig. 32 Grinding preform edges

no movement of the wrist as grinding is carried out. This will ensure that grinding follows the straight lines marked on the stone with the aluminium pencil. Round, oval, and other curved shapes must be held with equal firmness, but your wrist must be swung left and right in a gentle arc which follows the curved pencil line. Endeavour to develop a very light touch when using grinding wheels as this will greatly prolong their working lives.

When the edges of your preforms have been roughly shaped, the faces of the stones should also be passed once or twice across the coarse wheel in order to remove some of the blade marks made during slabbing. Do not overdo this face grinding otherwise the tumbled appearance of the finished preforms might be lost. The aim is to reduce the time it takes to polish the preforms in the tumbler by removing the deeper imperfections on the grinding wheel; but too much work at the wheel can spoil the final appearance of the piece.

Fig. 33 Grinding straight-sided and rounded preforms

straight-sided preform

preform is moved left and right across wheel with no wrist movement

curved preform

wrists swing in arc as preform is passed across wheel

When you have sufficient roughly ground preforms to half fill the tumbler, place them in the barrel and add a number of small pebbles to bring the load up to just under three-quarters full. These added pebbles will help to carry the silicon carbide to the flat faces of the preforms and greatly improve tumbling efficiency. Add the correct amount of coarse grit and proceed with the first stage of the tumbling operation as outlined in *Pebble Polishing*.

The grinding time will be approximately half that for a load of beach pebbles, and when your daily inspection confirms that most of the preforms have had all traces of diamond blade marks removed you can clean out the barrel and proceed to second stage grinding using fine silicon carbide grit. Again, this pre-polishing stage should take half the time required with a barrel containing beach pebbles. When daily inspection reveals that most of the preforms have a perfectly smooth matt finish you can wash out the barrel and remove the pebbles which you added to make up the load. Thoroughly wash the preforms and inspect each one carefully. Some will have cracked or chipped badly during the grinding stages and they must be rejected now. Others may have minor imperfections which will have to be removed before the polishing stage commences. This can usually be done with a few quick passes across the face of the fine wheel on your grinder.

When this hand-finishing has been carried out, wash all the preforms once again before placing them in the barrel for the final polish. This time the load should be made up to three-quarters by adding some leather off-cuts or small pieces of felt to the barrel. They will help to carry the polish to the flat surfaces of the preforms and also reduce the possibility of further breakages during the final run. Add the correct amount of water and cerium oxide and proceed with the polishing stage.

Angular preforms can be used quite effectively with bell caps to make unusual bracelets and pendants, but most preforms are used with flat pad jewellery fittings to make such things as cufflinks and tie-bars (*see* Plate 7). Flat squares and oblongs are also used for inlay work on trinket

Using preforms in jewellery-making

Fig. 34 Cutting a stone on
a horizontal unit

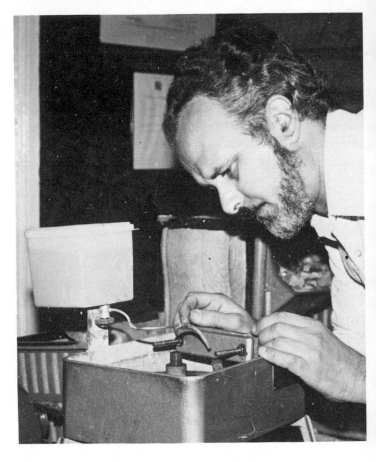

boxes and other small ornaments. Striking 'sculptures' can also be made by bonding preforms on to polished slabs with epoxy resin.

Of all the pleasing shapes and delightful specimens which amateur lapidaries produce in their home gem-cutting workshops cabochons are by far the most popular. The making of these 'beetle-backed' gemstones, so often seen in rings, pendants, bracelets and other items of jewellery, is a relatively simple task and one which is guaranteed to provide hours of pleasure and beautiful results. The skills you have already acquired in slabbing, trimming and making preforms are all used in cabochon cutting, and your familiarity with diamond saws and grinding wheels makes the task of producing your first 'cab' that much easier.

Before we go on to discuss the various steps in shaping the stone I want to introduce you to another machine which can be used in cabochon-making This is the horizontal

5 How to cut a cabochon

Machines

Fig. 35 You can cut, grind and polish stones on this horizontal unit

sawing, grinding, sanding and polishing unit: a machine which is relatively inexpensive and easy to use. Like the lapping machine it consists of an open tank in which a spindle or shaft is driven by means of pulleys and drive belt, fitted underneath the tank, which are in turn connected to an electric motor at the rear of the machine. A diamond sawblade is first mounted horizontally on the shaft and the drive belt positioned to give the fastest running speed. The stone to be cut or slabbed is held in a vice which can be raised or lowered on a vertical metal rod at the side of the machine. To cut the stone the vice is swung towards the rim of the blade and, with the water soluble coolant supply directed by means of a plastic tube onto the cutting rim, the stone is pressed against the blade and the cut completed. The vice is then lowered slightly and a second cut made to produce a slab.

Having cut the slab, the diamond blade is removed from the shaft and replaced by a coarse silicon carbide grinding wheel on which the stone is roughly shaped. A finer grinding wheel then replaces the coarse wheel on the shaft and the stone is brought to final shape. Next, a sanding disc is placed on the shaft and the drive belt moved to a pulley which provides a medium speed of revolution. All scratch marks on the stone are then gradually removed.

Finally, the sanding disc is replaced by a felt polishing pad which is charged with cerium oxide paste and the stone is brought to a high polish with the spindle turning at its slowest speed. Thus, by placing different attachments on a single shaft and by adjusting running speeds with various pulley sizes the tasks of sawing, grinding, sanding and polishing are carried out on a single machine.

Cabochons from pebbles

Returning to cabochons, your first attempts at producing these attractive gemstones should be made by slicing several symmetrically shaped pebbles on your trim saw or with the horizontal saw described above. If you use pebbles which have already been tumble-polished, your cabochons can be completed with a few minutes work on coarse and fine grinding wheels to smooth their rough edges and remove

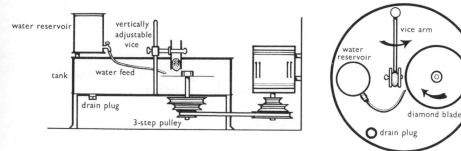

Fig. 36   A horizontal combination unit

blade marks from their bases. The only problem you will face when making jewellery with cabochons produced in this way is that of finding fittings into which the stones can be set. This is an easy problem to solve if you use the flat pad fittings normally used with baroque stones, but fittings designed for use with cabochons are made in a number of exact sizes. Unless you are extremely fortunate in the range of tumbled stones in your stocks the cabochons will be too large or too small for the fittings.

It is safer to start with an unpolished pebble which can be sliced and then ground to the correct size on a coarse silicon carbide wheel. First you must buy a plastic template stamped out with round and oval shapes in sizes which correspond to those of fittings made for cabochons. These sizes are expressed in millimetres, and each hole of your template will have its length and width clearly marked so that you can select the size to match your fitting.

Fig. 37   Typical cabochon fittings showing exact size requirement of shaped stone

Choose a pebble slightly larger than the hole in the template which corresponds to the size of jewellery fitting you wish to use. Slice the pebble on your trim saw and select the half which has the most pleasing surface appearance and the fewest flaws and imperfections. The base of this half must now be ground absolutely flat. This is best done on a cast-iron lapping unit using Nos. 80 and 220 silicon carbide grits, but if you do not own a lapping unit you can work the stone lightly across the sides of your coarse and fine grinding wheels. This should only be done to remove minor imperfections left by the diamond blade. *The sides of your grinding wheels should never be used for heavy grinding work.*

When the base is absolutely flat, place your plastic template on it and mark the circumference of the cabochon with an aluminium pencil. Ensure that the point of the pencil marks a line as close as possible to the edge of the template hole by holding the pencil at an angle when scribing. If you hold the pencil vertically the shape drawn will be much smaller than the hole in the template.

The next task is to grind the edges of the pebble until they correspond with the line you have marked. This is done on the coarse grinding wheel. Hold the stone with the flat side uppermost and with your fingers supporting the rounded portion underneath. Place your thumbs on the flat base and present the stone to the edge of the grinding wheel. Work in the centre of the wheel and move your wrists to left and right throughout the grinding operation. At the same time the stone must be slowly turned in your hands so that the edge is worn down evenly around the base until the pencil line is reached. You will probably find that a sludge of stone dust and water tends to build up on the edge of the stone, especially when a large amount of waste material must be removed. To prevent this, have a bowl of water nearby and dip the pebble into it frequently during the operation. The water drip feed must, of course, be maintained on the wheels at all times; and do remember the correct procedure for starting and stopping the motor and turning the water supply on and off.

Plate 1   Stones which can be found in Britain

| Smoky quartz (Cairngorm) | | Agate | Red jasper |
| Citrine | Amethyst | Jet | Agate |

Plate 2   Larger rocks which can be cut and used for jewellery-making

| Rhodonite | | | Amethyst |
| Rhodocrosite | Polished tiger eye | | Rough tiger eye |

Plate 3   Imported rocks, available from lapidary suppliers in Britain

Rough sodalite	Polished sodalite	Aventurine
Polished Queensland agate (slab)	Rough Queensland agate	Chrysoprase
		Moonstone
Rough Queensland agate		Labradorite
Rose quartz (polished and unpolished)		Lapis lazuli
	Bloodstone	Amazonite

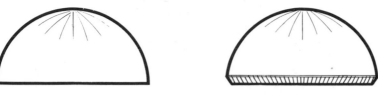

To complete the base of the stone, the sharp edge formed where the flat face meets the sloping sides must be smoothed by grinding a narrow bevel or chamfer around the base. The purpose of this sloping edge is to avoid any splintering of the base during the shaping of the dome, and also to ensure that the finished cabochon will fit neatly into the jewellery mount. The chamfer is easily formed by passing the edge of the base across the grinding wheel at the same angle as you would work when sharpening a knife blade.

Fig. 38 Shaped stone before and after grinding of chamfer around base

Dopping the stone

With the work on the base completed you must now grind, sand and polish the dome. Coarse grinding can be carried out while holding the stone in your hands if it is a fairly large cabochon. This is the usual procedure when using a horizontal grinding wheel, but smaller stones and those which are to be shaped on vertical wheels are easier to hold if they are now attached to dop sticks. Dopping simply means attaching a handle to the base of the stone to make it easier to manipulate, and a dop stick is an ordinary piece of dowel about 5 in. long with a flat end slightly narrower than the base of the stone. Call at your local timber shop and buy half a dozen lengths of dowel in sizes ranging from $\frac{1}{4}$–$\frac{3}{4}$ in.; take them home and cut them into 5-in. lengths with perfectly straight saw cuts and you will have sufficient dop sticks to last a lifetime.

The time-honoured method of attaching the stone to the stick is to use dop wax, and like many such methods it is the best—if you carry out the job correctly. You will be able to buy a dopping unit at your rock shop, or you can make yourself a simple stove with the following items:

Fig. 39 A dopping unit sold
by many rock shops

2 empty bean cans (largest size)
1 empty bean can (smallest size)
1 empty can about half the size of your small bean can
flat metal tray
a 2-in. stub of candle
dop sticks
stick of dop wax (available for a few pence at your
rock shop)

The dop wax is broken into pieces and placed in the
smallest can, the small bean can is punctured on its bottom

and sides with as many holes as you can make with a 6-inch nail and hammer, the two large bean cans are filled almost to overflowing with sand, and the metal tray is wiped clean, dried, and placed conveniently nearby. Light the candle and place the punctured bean can over it. Put the smallest can containing the dop wax onto this miniature stove and keep a careful watch until the wax begins to melt. *It must not be allowed to boil and bubble.* If it should do so extinguish the candle immediately by blowing through the holes in the can. Have two or three dop sticks of various thicknesses in your hands and rest their ends on the top of the stove so that the wood is warmed. When you see that the wax has melted, dip each stick into it to a depth of half an inch. Turn the stick in your fingers for a few moments then withdraw it smoothly from the wax and stand it on end on the flat tray. The wax will run down the stick towards the tray and form a conical, flat-topped bed on which your stone will rest evenly.

Prepare several dop sticks in this way while the wax is molten. As their ends harden on the metal tray they can be removed and stored, wax upwards, in the sand tins until required. Take care that the wax in the melting pot does not become too hot during your dopping operations. It will lose its ability to adhere to your stones if it is allowed to boil. Control the temperature by extinguishing and re-lighting the candle.

With a supply of waxed sticks in your sand tins you can now dop one of your half-made cabochons. The stone must first be warmed by placing its flat side *upwards* on the candle stove. It will have reached the correct temperature when you can just bear to place your finger on the flat base. Select a dop stick slightly narrower than the base and pass it slowly over the candle stove so that the wax begins to soften. Now, with a swift but smooth movement, press the flat face of the wax against the flat face of the stone and lift it from the top of the stove. Turn the dop stick so that the stone is resting squarely on the top, moisten your fingers by licking them, and gently centralize the stone as you mould the soft wax around its base to form a solid

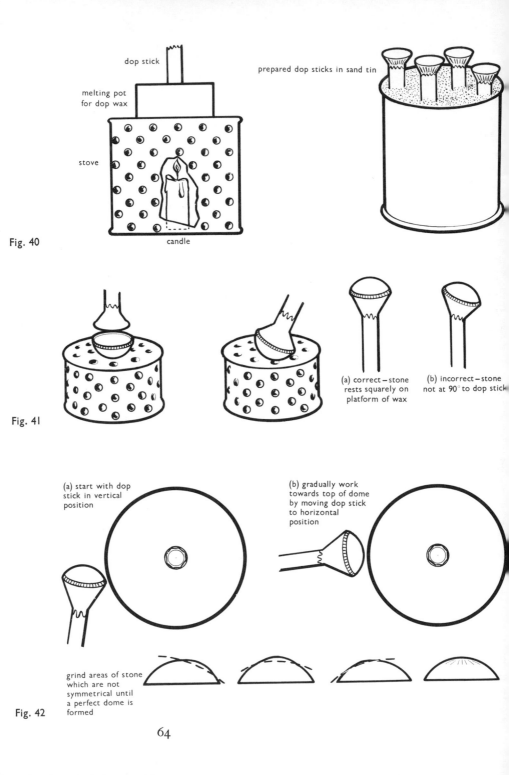

dop stick

prepared dop sticks in sand tin

melting pot
for dop wax

stove

candle

Fig. 40

(a) correct – stone
rests squarely on
platform of wax

(b) incorrect – stone
not at 90° to dop stick

Fig. 41

(a) start with dop
stick in vertical
position

(b) gradually work
towards top of dome
by moving dop stick
to horizontal
position

grind areas of stone
which are not
symmetrical until
a perfect dome is
formed

Fig. 42

platform. Return the mounted stone to the sand tin until the wax has hardened when your cabochon will be ready for grinding, sanding and polishing.

Commence on the coarse grinding wheel after examining the stone carefully to decide at which points the shape is not symmetrical. Bring the dome into contact with the wheel slightly below the centre of the rim; sweep it back and forth across the face, at the same time rotating the dop stick between fingers and thumb. Start with the stick in a near vertical position and gradually work towards the horizontal. When turning the stone on the stick you should increase pressure when those areas which are not symmetrical are in contact with the wheel. The aim is to form a perfect dome without flats or ridges.

Shaping the dome

When you are satisfied with the shape of the dome, wash the stone thoroughly in clean water and proceed to the fine grinding wheel. Go over the entire surface once again in the same manner. At this stage a very light touch is required in order to avoid the grinding of tiny flats. Keep the stone moving across the wheel and rotate the dop stick rapidly in your fingers. When all coarse grinding scratches have been removed wash the stone again in preparation for the next stage.

Sanding is carried out on the vertical sanding disc at the end of your machine. Attach a No. 320 silicon carbide paper-backed sanding sheet to the rubber-faced disc and move the drive belt on the pulleys to give a medium running speed. Use a plastic bottle to apply water to the sheet as it spins, and bear in mind that the aim in sanding is to remove scratches left on the surface of the stone by the fine grinding wheel. Keep the stone moving and roll it across the spinning disc on the dop stick. Change to a No. 400 sheet to produce

Fig. 40 (*top*) Candle stove for dopping stones

Fig. 41 (*centre*) Lifting warmed stone on prepared dop stick

Fig. 42 (*bottom*) Shaping the dome

an absolutely smooth matt finish on the cabochon dome and ensure an adequate supply of water from the bottle throughout the entire sanding stage.

Final polishing is carried out at the other end of the machine using the felt pad, but before polishing commences wash the dopped stone and your hands very carefully to remove all traces of silicon carbide. Move the drive belt on the pulleys to provide the slowest running speed and then apply a thin paste of cerium oxide and water to the pad as it spins and spread it evenly across the surface. Do not saturate the polishing disc with water. It must remain moist throughout the polishing stage, but too much water will cause the cerium oxide to fly from the pad. Rotate the dome of the cabochon across the moist face of the pad for a few minutes and you should produce a mirror finish on the stone.

When satisfied with the polish achieved you can remove the finished cabochon from the dop stick by holding it firmly between your fingers and giving a quick sideways pull. If this should fail place the dopped stone in the freezer compartment of your refrigerator for five minutes and then try again. The wax will contract when cold and the stone should then drop off.

It should be noted that the sanding and polishing stages of forming the cabochon can, of course, be carried out on the horizontal machine already described, or on a lapping unit using loose Nos. 320 and 400 grits and cerium oxide. The procedure for working the stone is identical to that used with vertical sanding and polishing discs.

Cabochons from slabs Because they are already dome-shaped, sliced beach pebbles are ideal material for beginners with little experience of grinding wheels. Once you have gained some experience at forming symmetrical domes you can proceed to cutting cabochons from slabbed stone and produce even more beautiful specimens. Remember when cutting or buying your slabs that they must be parallel-sided and slightly thicker than the height of the finished cabochon to allow for waste when grinding. They must also be free from cracks

66

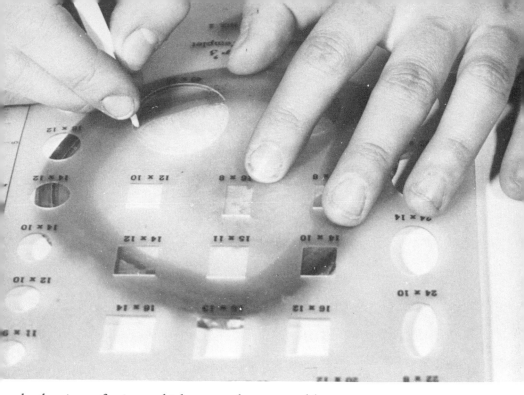

and other imperfections which cannot be removed later.

Remove all saw blade marks on a flat lap with loose silicon carbide grit and mark out the cabochon shape with a template and aluminium pencil. The trim saw is used to cut the slab into smaller shapes and to remove as much waste as possible from the trimmed slab. All cuts with the blade must be absolutely straight, and an allowance for the thickness of the blade must be made when trimming. Coarse grinding of the cabochon outline can be carried out with the trimmed slab held in the hands. The method is the same as described for grinding oval preforms, but with cabochons the slab can be held slightly above the centre of the wheel so that the walls are ground with a slightly inward curve. Keep the stone moving across the face of the wheel and when the outline is completed grind a narrow chamfer on the sharp edge. The stone is now ready for dopping. Follow the instructions given for dopping sliced pebbles, and bear in mind that it is the face with the chamfered edge which is attached to the dop stick.

Fig. 43 Marking cabochon shapes on a flat slab with the aid of a template

67

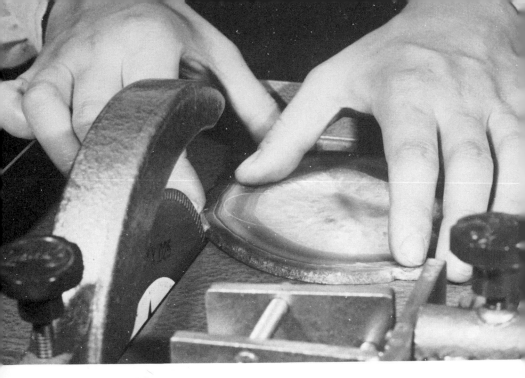

Fig. 44   Trimming the slab
to a rough cabochon shape

Fig. 45   Grinding the
cabochon

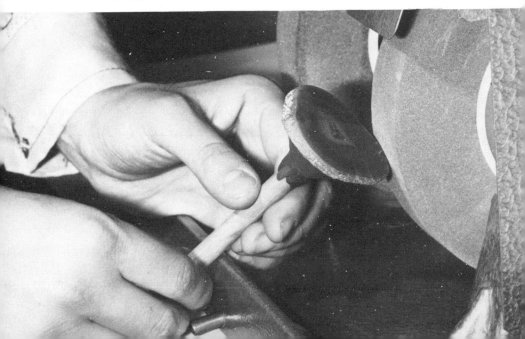

Fig. 46 A small, well designed unit for cabochon making. It has a vertical saw at one end of the shaft, while the grinding, sanding and polishing wheels can be mounted at the other end

Again, the procedure is as for pebble slices, greater care being taken to avoid the grinding of flats during preliminary shaping. Do not make sudden changes to the angle at which the stone is held against the grinding wheel. The aim should be to gradually round the outer walls towards the centre of the stone to produce a perfect dome. Proceed to sanding and polishing only after you have achieved a perfectly smooth cabochon outline with the grinding wheels.

Grinding, sanding and polishing

Fig. 47 The hand-held slab is presented to the grinding wheel slightly above centre line to produce inward-curving sides. The slab is then reversed before dopping

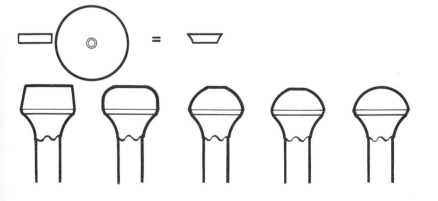

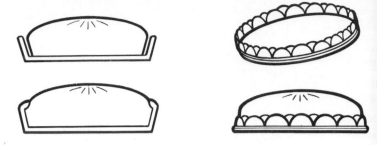

Fig. 48 Plain and fancy
cabochon fittings

Jewellery-making with cabochons

Jewellery fittings for use with cabochons differ from the flat pad fittings used with baroque stones by having a raised edge which is rubbed over the stone after it has been cemented in position to give a neat and attractive finish to the piece. The raised edge might be plain or fancy in style and the variety of cabochon fittings is extremely wide. Rings, brooches, cufflinks, pendants and earrings can all be made using cabochons of many different shapes. When buying your fittings ensure that they are of the size to match the cabochons you plan to cut. Mail order catalogues for home jewellery-making equipment always state in millimetres the size of cabochon required for a particular fitting.

In spite of the enormous range of manufactured fittings which home jewellery makers can buy, and the simple efficiency of epoxy resin as an adhesive for bonding gemstones to jewellery mounts, almost every newcomer to the hobby wants to drill a hole in a stone. I believe this is because most absolute beginners imagine that necklaces, pendants and other pieces of jewellery produced by amateur lapidaries are made with drilled stones. They soon realize that this is not so and that drilled stones are only very occasionally used by home jewellery makers. Nevertheless the desire to drill holes in semi-precious stones persists.

Until quite recently the cost of equipment suitable for drilling holes in obdurate stone was so high that most amateur lapidaries were content to leave this branch of the subject to professional workers in commercial lapidary establishments. If they required a drilled stone for a particular item of jewellery, this was either purchased ready-drilled or the stone was taken to a professional who provided a hole-drilling service. Today, thanks to the introduction of inexpensive, battery-operated drilling machines and to the availability of diamond-tipped drillbits the job can be successfully tackled by amateur lapidaries at a fairly reasonable cost per hole. However, you should ask yourself before buying the tools whether the cost of the equipment required is justified by the number of holes you wish to drill. If you own a trim saw you can cut a neat slot in the edge of a stone into which a jump ring can be cemented. This will serve

6 Drilling a hole in a stone

Equipment

Fig. 49 Two methods of mounting a polished slab

drilled stone

(b) slit stone — cut is made with a trim saw and bolt ring is cemented in position

equally well on almost every occasion you might need a drilled stone for a pendant or necklace. A little imagination used in the creation of other items of jewellery can usually overcome the lack of hole-drilling facilities in your workshop, and the range of manufactured fittings for use with epoxy resin continues to grow. In spite of this you may still feel that a drilling machine is essential, so we will now look briefly at how holes are drilled.

I must stress that special equipment is needed. *You cannot drill gemstones with home power tools used for carpentry or metalwork.* Such machines run at a speed of approximately 2,000 r.p.m. and this is much too slow for gemstone drilling. Furthermore, the drillbits used to drill wood and metal are cutting tools which remove waste material as shavings as the hole is drilled; whereas diamond-tipped lapidary drillbits are really cylindrical grinding wheels with a large number of abrasive points which remove waste material as tiny granular particles.

A small drilling machine with a speed of up to 9,000 r.p.m. and capable of being run on a 12 volt battery can be purchased for less than the price of a home power tool. You will also need a drill stand in which to mount the machine to ensure absolutely accurate drilling. The stand will cost slightly more than the drilling machine, but it must be regarded as essential equipment if you are to avoid breaking the expensive diamond bits.

There are two types of drillbit on the market. The first, which is the least expensive, has a single layer of diamond particles deposited on its shank, and its obvious disadvantage is that once this layer has been removed the drill's working life is at an end. The second type has many layers of diamond particles bonded on its shank and it can, therefore, be used to drill many more holes before a new drill must be purchased. As the top layer of diamonds become worn or blunted fresh diamond points are exposed to prolong drilling efficiency. Initially this type of drillbit costs more than the plated variety, but with careful use it should prove a more economical proposition.

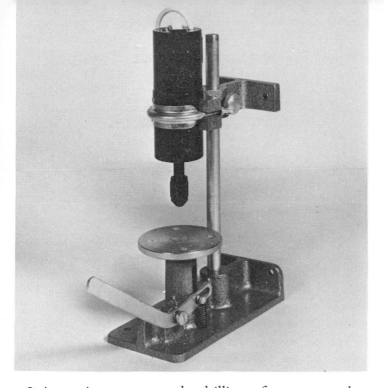

Fig. 50 The Expo drill and stand suitable for lapidary drilling work

Drilling the hole

It is unwise to attempt the drilling of any stone other than a flat slab because of the difficulty experienced in starting the drill on a curved surface. Drill your holes in preforms *before* you grind and polish them and your drill-bits will last much longer. Only thin slabs should be drilled; any slab more than $\frac{1}{2}$ in. in thickness should not be used. Mark out the template shape and cut the piece to rough shape on your trim saw before deciding where you will drill the hole. Mark this spot with your aluminium pencil

Fig. 51 (*left*) Drillbit detail
Fig. 52 (*right*) Drilling without a drill stand can ruin an expensive drillbit

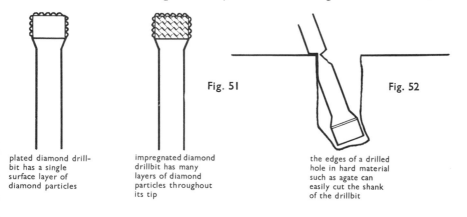

Fig. 51

Fig. 52

plated diamond drill-bit has a single surface layer of diamond particles

impregnated diamond drillbit has many layers of diamond particles throughout its tip

the edges of a drilled hole in hard material such as agate can easily cut the shank of the drillbit

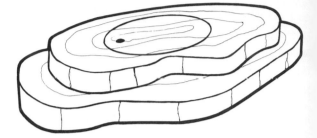

Fig. 53 Marked workpiece
temporarily glued to a
piece of waste slab

and then temporarily glue the preform to a similarly sized
piece of waste slab. This is necessary in order to prevent
fractures around the drilled hole as the bit breaks through
the back of the workpiece.

You will now need a small, flat-bottomed plastic or glass
container into which the prepared stone can be placed.
(Plastic tops from aerosol spray cans are ideal.) Put the
workpiece into this container and pour in clean water until
the top of the stone is covered to a depth of approximately
$\frac{1}{8}$ in. After providing the correct power supply, mounting
the drill in the stand, and fixing the drillbit in the chuck
according to the manufacturer's instructions, the plastic
container should be placed on the stand and the drillbit
aligned with the point on the stone where you wish to drill
the hole.

Fig. 54 A plastic water
container holding work-
piece is positioned beneath
the drillbit

Drilling is carried out with a series of very short runs by
the bit. Bring the drill into contact with the stone for 2 or

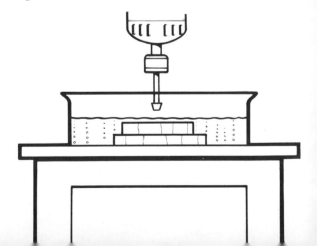

3 seconds and then withdraw the bit so that water can reach the bottom of the hole to reduce the temperature and wash out the cuttings. As the hole deepens, the drilling time should be reduced to 1 or 2 seconds while the length of time for which the bit is withdrawn from the hole should be increased. It is a slow process, particularly when drilling very hard material such as agate; it may take up to 15 minutes to make a single hole in a slab. On no account must you attempt to speed up the process by keeping the bit in contact with the stone for long periods. You will damage the drill irreparably if you do so.

Some stones are so resistant to drilling that it becomes necessary to sharpen the diamond bit halfway through the cut. To do this remove the plastic container and drill a hole into a piece of discarded No. 220 silicon carbide grinding wheel. This will dress the face of your diamond drillbit and restore it to peak cutting efficiency.

7 Simple faceting

A faceted gemstone has a number of flat planes, or facets, cut symmetrically across its surface, and when these are polished, rays of light which fall upon them are reflected and refracted to enhance the fire and brilliance of the gem. The professional facet cutter who works with diamonds, sapphires and other precious gems possesses a considerable knowledge of physics and mathematics; he spends many years perfecting the techniques of his craft to produce gems of great beauty. Often he will study a gemstone for several days before deciding to facet it in a particular way so that its hidden beauty may be revealed to the best advantage. He is, indeed, a Master Craftsman.

How then can you, a newcomer to amateur lapidary, hope to facet your semi-precious stones successfully? In fact, so long as you are prepared to accept that the simple faceting we are about to attempt with some inexpensive attachments used on one of the machines already described in this book is somewhat removed from the world of the professional facet cutter, you can certainly emulate his skills and produce quite delightful faceted semi-precious stones. They may lack the technical brilliance of the gems cut from precious stones, but they will give you hours of pleasure in the making and endless satisfaction when you display them to the admiration of relatives and friends. Later, as your lapidary skills develop, you may decide to purchase a precision faceting machine which, with long practice, will enable you to develop professional skills.

Meanwhile, we will return to the cast-iron lapping machine discussed in Chapter 3. As you know, this machine is used to produce an absolutely flat surface on a slab with the aid of loose silicon carbide grits. If you were to take a beach pebble and work it across the flat lap using No. 80 silicon carbide grit, you would grind a flat on the oval pebble and this flat would, in fact, be a facet. If you then turned the pebble slightly between your fingers and proceeded to grind a second flat adjacent to the first a faceted stone would begin to take shape. If additional flats were produced around the first one you would end up with a crudely faceted stone.

76

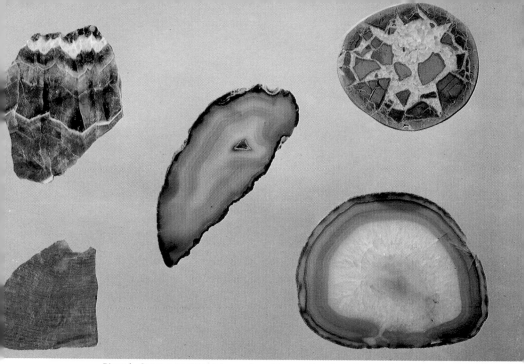

Plate 4   Some beautiful slabs ready-cut by suppliers from imported rocks

Phantom amethyst

Brazilian agate

Septarian nodule

Petrified wood

Brazilian agate

Plate 5   Delightful examples of faceted stones

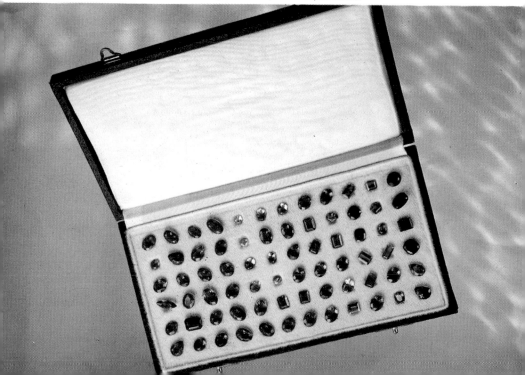

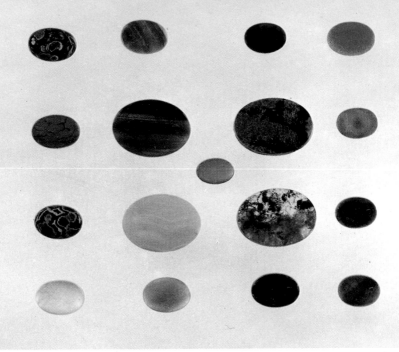

Plate 6   A selection of cabochons

Plate 7   Some jewellery which can be made with cabochons

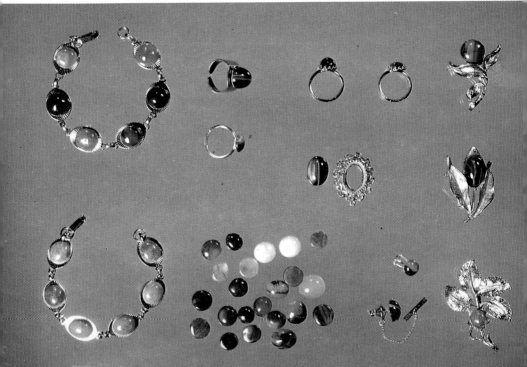

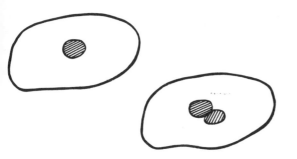

The finished stone would look crude only because the facets were formed with the stone held between your fingers; you would be unable to position the stone accurately on the lap so that facets were formed symmetrically around its surface. In order to position the stone accurately on the lap you require a faceting attachment.

This consists of a vertical metal rod mounted at the side

Fig. 55 A crudely faceted pebble

Fig. 56 Simple faceting attachments for an 8-inch lap

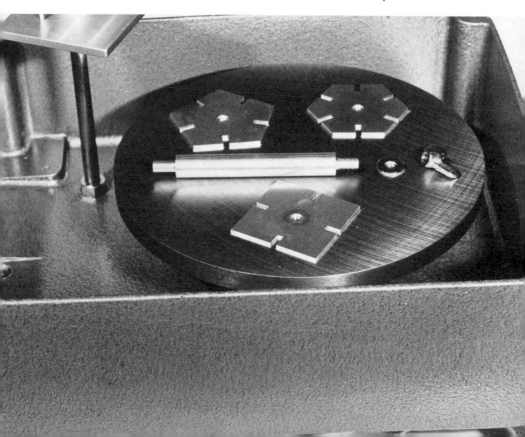

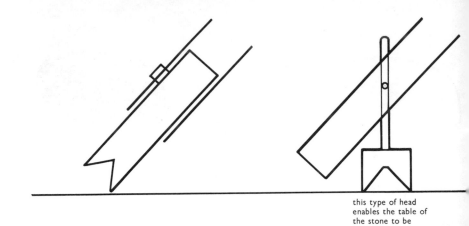

this type of head
enables the table of
the stone to be
accurately ground

Fig. 57 Dopstick heads of the lap tank on which a flat worktable can be raised or lowered and locked at any height. On this worktable a metal former, or template, of symmetrical shape is rested. It has a central hole through which a metal dop stick of sufficient length to reach the flat lap can be screwed.

The dop stick is rather special. It has several removable heads to take stones of different sizes, and on some units a head can be attached at an angle of 45° so that the flat top, or table, of the gem can be ground. On other units this table is formed with the dop stick held in a free-hand **Fig. 58 Grinding a rough** position. Some of the dop stick heads are partly hollowed **preform** or recessed to enable the preformed stone to be dopped

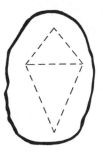   

required shape   roughly ground   finished preform   preform in dop stick

78

squarely and accurately, and also to provide better adhesion between stone and dop stick.

You can, as we have seen, facet a baroque pebble by holding it in your hand. You can also facet slabs and cabochons in the same way to produce interesting lozenge-shaped stones. But best results are achieved if you preform a rough stone so that it can be held in one of the recessed dop stick heads in order to produce geometrically accurate facets.

The shape required is rather like an old-fashioned spinning top or two pyramids—one about half the height of the other—joined at their bases. This can be roughly formed on your coarse grinding wheel so that the apex of the largest pyramid fits into one of the recessed heads. It must then be carefully dopped as outlined in Chapter 5, care being taken to ensure that the stone sits squarely and securely in the recessed dop.

Preforming the stone

The first task is to produce the flat top, or table, of the faceted gem. Prepare the lap as for grinding a flat slab, using a paste of water and No. 220 silicon carbide grit, and grind the table by holding the dop stick perpendicular to the lap.

When a suitable table has been ground lift the stone from the lap and switch off the machine. Now select one of your templates and secure this to the top of the dop stick. Rest

Faceting or forming the stone

Fig. 59 Symmetrical facets

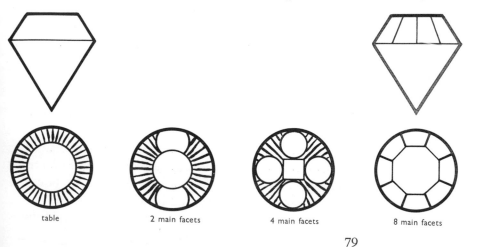

table   2 main facets   4 main facets   8 main facets

the template on the worktable so that the side of your stone is in contact with the stationary cast-iron lap and move the worktable up or down on the vertical rod until the stone is at the angle required on the lap. When you have decided on the angle at which you will cut your facets, secure the worktable at the selected height and lift the dopped stone from the lap *before* you switch on the motor once again. Now bring the dop stick gently into contact with the lap so that the stone is ground *in the direction of rotation.*

When a facet has been formed lift the dop and rotate the template on the worktable to the next flat. Bring the stone into contact with the lap once again and grind the next facet, continuing in this way until facets have been formed symmetrically around the table.

The next step is to repeat the entire process, including the grinding of the table, using No. 400 grit. Do not move the worktable on the vertical rod, otherwise you will have difficulty in placing the stone on the lap at the same angle used during the previous grinding stage. The polishing stage, using cerium oxide, follows the fine grind.

With the grinding and polishing of the table and main facets completed, the stone must be removed from its dop stick and re-dopped on a flat-ended dop head using the table as the base of the stone. The faceting of the lower portion, or pavilion, of the stone is then carried out as described above.

We have dealt with the simple faceting of semi-precious stones using a cast-iron lapping machine, but it should be noted that similar faceting attachments are also available for use with the horizontal combination unit described in Chapter 5. Copper laps impregnated with diamond particles are also available for use on a number of horizontal machines, though they are more likely to be used with an advanced faceting unit.

Manufactured fittings for faceted gemstones are not readily available, but I feel sure this will not deter you from producing faceted stones which can look really beautiful when simply displayed against a background of rich velvet. If you wish to use the stones in pad or cabochon fittings

you can grind a flat on the lower portion of the stone so
that it fits neatly into the mount.

Fig. 60 A reasonably
priced, advanced faceting
machine

Fig. 61 Faceting terms

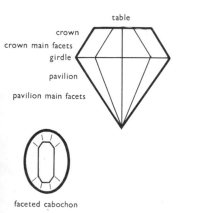

table

crown

crown main facets

girdle

pavilion

pavilion main facets

faceted cabochon

pavilion ground flat
so that stone can be
attached to standard
fitting

faceted slab

8 Gem collecting

Having whetted your appetites with the title of this chapter, let me now say a few words to those readers who imagine that after reading the next few pages they will no longer need to visit their local rock shops to buy rough material to cut and grind on their machines. The specimens you *may* find by following the rules set out below are most unlikely to compare with the excellent rough gems on sale in rock shops unless you happen to live in North America or Australia—countries renowned for their spectacular gems. Such readers are to be envied. The basic geological rules set out here apply no matter where they are used, and all overseas readers will benefit from learning them.

British readers may find consolation in the fact that diamonds, sapphires, gold and giant-size semi-precious crystals *have* been found in Britain; and that within these islands almost every known geological formation, rare mineral and precious gem can be found. This chapter is written for those adventurous souls prepared to risk disappointment, enjoy the scenery, and perhaps take home a few specimens for a collecting cabinet. I hope that some of you will take home gemstones worthy of faceting, or at least of cabochon cutting, but you must remember that the best gemstones in Britain are to be found in the High Street where your local lapidary dealer has his premises.

There is nothing difficult about finding semi-precious stones in Britain. Spend an off-season weekend at any seaside resort in Scotland, Cornwall or the east coast of England and wander, eyes down, along the deserted shingle beaches. Keep at it throughout Saturday and Sunday, your mind as well as your eyes on the pebbles beneath your feet, and pick up every brightly coloured or shining specimens you see. By late Sunday afternoon a pound or two of attractive pebbles should be in your collecting bag—and some of them will almost certainly be amethyst, cairngorm, citrine, agate, amber, cornelian or jet.

That's how easy it is when you know where to look, and you are prepared to be patient and to use your powers of observation. It is a formula for success which works equally well if you apply it to a hunt for semi-precious gems on the high, wild moors, hills and mountains we are about to discuss. You may not find all the specimens a trained geologist would locate if he covered the same stretches of countryside; and I am not suggesting that a knowledge of geology is quite unnecessary in order to become a successful rockhound. A little knowledge is certainly *not* a bad thing when it comes to hunting semi-precious rocks and minerals. The few geological clues set out here are very likely to guide you to at least some of the crystal specimens and gems which lie hidden in many areas of Britain; and they are unconditionally guaranteed to guide you to some of the most spectacular scenery within these islands. Shortcomings in geological expertise can be more than made up by improving your powers of observation, and by possessing the patience to keep looking when the less determined have given up and gone home empty-handed.

1 *Keep out of danger.* Heathery moors, magnificent mountains and craggy rock faces far from the hustle and bustle of city life have given delight, excitement and the pleasures of solitude to millions of people. In summertime they are the adventure playgrounds of the great outdoors where your rockhounding excursions will be as safe as a day trip to Margate or Blackpool. Be warned, however, that in winter such places change their characters as dramatically as Doctor Jekyll changed to Mister Hyde.

An acquaintance of mine who ventured into the wilds of Sutherland in mid winter on a gold-prospecting expedition lost his tent and sleeping bag when a mountain stream suddenly changed course. He spent several days in hospital recovering from frostbite. Another, caught in a November snowstorm on the North Yorkshire Moors, where he was hunting freshwater pearls, sprained an ankle and lost most of his equipment when he fell into a moorland stream which had been blanketed by a snowdrift. He was saved from severe exposure only by his good fortune in stumbling upon a lonely farmhouse.

Both of these men were experienced treasure hunters who had spent many winters in mountainous regions and they

The rules for success

had taught themselves the rules of survival when Nature turns nasty. Yet even they came very close to losing their lives. The message is absolutely clear: confine your rock-hounding to the months of May, June, July and August.

Long abandoned mine workings are familiar sites in the regions you will visit. You are certain to be fascinated by the old equipment and derelict buildings often found near them where the ghosts of a long-dead prosperity still seem to linger. Some make delightful settings for picnics on family outings, and there are excellent prospects of finding exciting gem material in the overgrown spoil heaps which will surround the site. Search them by all means; but *please* do not enter the abandoned mine shaft no matter how safe it appears when viewed from the surface. The chances of finding gem specimens in the old workings are poor: most of the worthwhile material will have long ago been thrown on to the spoil heap by the miners who followed the mineral lode. The chances of a fall, however, are extremely high if you venture into the shaft. Again, the message is clear: stick to the spoil heaps where the best finds await you.

Working mines and quarries can also be dangerous places, especially those where explosives are used. Blasting often weakens walls and falls of rock can occur. Keep away unless you have obtained permission to search spoil heaps from a responsible person in charge of operations.

2 *Carry the right equipment.* The absolute essential is a geological hammer. Gem crystals are often called 'flowers of the rocks'—but you cannot pluck them with your bare hands. You must have the correct tool for the job. There are two basic types of hammer. The first has a pointed tip on one side of the hammer head and is known as a *pick head*; the other has a flat edge instead of a point and is known as a *chisel head*.

If you wish to keep the amount of equipment you have to carry to an absolute minimum the chisel head is probably best. On the other hand, there are some excellent small chisels available which are ideal for the often delicate job of extracting crystals from rock. Small chisels from your own

84

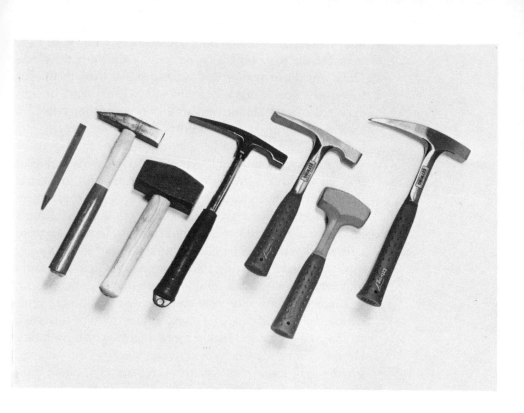

tool box might also be suitable, in which case it is better to buy the pick head because it will provide you with an extra tool on the other side of the head.

Fig. 62 Rockhounding tools, available from many rock shops

A rucksack is next in order of importance. Gem-collecting locations cannot be reached by car, though you will be able to drive to within reasonable walking distance of many sites. Eventually, however, you will have to rely on your legs to carry you and your equipment over broken ground. You will also have a fair load in the way of collected specimens to carry back, and for this job a good quality rucksack is needed. The unframed types are generally lighter and less expensive, and they provide adequate storage space for everything needed on a one-day outing, with plenty of room to spare for your finds.

A one-inch Ordnance Survey map of the area you plan to visit and a reliable compass are also most important. Both are quite useless unless you know how to read them. Do not venture far into wild countryside until you have mastered the basic skills of map reading and compass work. Once you have mastered the basic skills, trust them. Far too many people have become lost when caught in unexpected mists or rainstorms simply because they relied on their 'sense of direction' instead of on their compasses.

Clothing for a day to be spent on high ground must be windproof yet comfortable to wear. Nylon shirts and jeans may be ideal for a stroll around a nearby tourist town, but they are useless and can be dangerous on hilltops where they quickly become wet and cold if the weather changes unexpectedly. Instead, select woollen shirts, loose-fitting and lightweight sweaters, woollen trousers or slacks, and a good quality anorak. A pair of stout walking shoes and fairly thick woollen socks will complete your rockhounding outfit.

'Luxury' items such as a thermos of hot soup, some sandwiches, a camera, and even a pair of binoculars are worth taking on a trip lasting more than two or three hours. Do remember, however, that overloading on the outward journey will result in a very tiring return trip. Plastic bags, a multi-bladed penknife, and perhaps some soft tissue paper to wrap any delicate specimens you find can be carried in the pockets of your anorak.

3 *Know which rocks to look for*. Hunting a needle in a haystack is not the impossible task most people believe it to be. A simple solution to the problem would be to burn the haystack to the ground and go over the ashes very carefully with a metal detector. You would probably find the needle —but you would then have to face the irate farmer.

A more scientific approach would be to find out as much as possible about the person who hid the needle in the first place. How tall was he? What was the length of his arm? Did he use a ladder to reach the upper part of the stack? Such scientific detective work would then enable you to eliminate large areas of the haystack and to concentrate your search on those places most likely to hold that elusive needle.

The same scientific approach can be made when hunting

semi-precious gems. Nature hid most of her prizes in or alongside certain types of rocks. If you can identify those rocks you will be able to concentrate your search in the most likely places and greatly increase your chances of making worthwhile finds. You will not discover every gem which Nature has hidden—you will still require patience and careful observation if you are to achieve any success at all—but you will certainly shorten the odds considerably in your favour if you take the trouble to familiarize yourself with the likely hiding places of many gems.

The rocks which hold the widest variety of gems and therefore interest us most are known as *igneous* rocks. They were formed many millions of years ago when red-hot molten substances which geologists call *magmas* rose upwards from deep within the bowels of the earth. Sometimes these molten magmas reached the surface as *lavas* which poured forth from volcanoes or from cracks within the earth's crust. Rocks formed from these lavas are known as *volcanic* or *extrusive* rocks.

Igneous rocks

Some molten magmas did not reach the surface, in spite of the enormous forces which pushed them upwards. Instead, they forced their way into other rocks beneath the surface where they then solidified. Igneous rocks formed in this way are known as *intrusive* or *plutonic* rocks. Millions of years later, when the overlying rocks had been worn away by the erosive action of the weather, or more recently when railway cuttings, quarries and road constructions removed their coverings, the intrusive or plutonic rocks were also exposed as outcrops on the surface.

Because they solidified underground, the intrusive rocks cooled slowly. This enabled them to develop relatively large mineral crystals which give intrusive rocks a typical coarse grained texture.

Granite is the best known example of the intrusive, coarse-grained rocks. If you look at a piece of granite closely you will see that it is composed of a jumbled mass of small crystals varying in size from $\frac{1}{16}$ in. to $\frac{1}{2}$ in.; and that it has a characteristic sparkle which is caused by tiny particles of mica between the crystals. Granite is typically light in colour, and may be white, grey, pink or yellowish brown. The size of its crystal grains is determined by how slowly the magma cooled beneath the earth's crust. In some granites known as *pegmatites* (*see* p. 94), which cooled very slowly, the crystals can measure many feet across; in others which cooled near the surface and therefore much quicker the crystals are quite small. But the common feature of all granites is their hardness which makes them ideal building and road-making materials. They occur widely in Britain, particularly in Cornwall, The Lake District, Caernarvonshire and Scotland.

Porphyry is a variety of granite in which bands of larger crystals stand out clearly. The Shap granite of Westmorland is a good example. It displays quite large crystals of pink feldspar.

Gabbro is a heavy, dark-coloured, coarse-grained rock which contains a green mineral known as olivine. The crystals in gabbro are usually dark green, grey or black. It is found mainly in Cornwall, Pembrokeshire, The Lake District and Scotland.

Syenite is a coarse-grained rock resembling granite, but darker in colour, and usually of a grey or reddish hue. It is found mainly in Caernarvonshire and Ireland.

Diorite is another rock resembling granite. It may be dark grey in colour, but often displays a green and white mottled effect to which it owes its commoner name of greenstone. It is found in Pembrokeshire.

The five rocks listed above—granite, porphyry, gabbro, syenite and diorite—are all coarse-grained intrusive rocks, and many of the gemstones we are seeking will be found in or near them. The fine-grained extrusive rocks contain fewer semi-precious specimens. Nevertheless, they are most worthy of our attention:

Basalt is the best known of the fine-grained extrusives. It is a heavy, compact rock which was formed when floods of lava poured from numerous cracks in the earth's crust and flowed over the surface before hardening. When some of these basalt lava flows cooled the rocks contracted and split into columnar structures which can be vividly seen in The Giant's Causeway on the coast of Northern Ireland. Some basalts contain numerous open spaces or pores which were caused when gas and steam bubbled out of the cooling lava. This porous basalt is known as *scoria*, and its mineral-filled pores often contain fine crystals.

Dolerite is very similar to basalt in its mineralogical make-up and appearance. Indeed, it is almost impossible to distinguish between the two when they are seen as small specimens in a geological cabinet, but dolerite is found under different conditions. When the molten lava solidified as a sheet or sill beneath a very thin covering of other rocks the result is dolerite. It is, therefore, an intrusive rock; but it cooled so near the surface that it is extremely fine-grained. The Great Whin Sill which runs across the north of England, and on which part of Hadrian's Wall stands, is the largest mass of dolerite in Britain.

Andesite is a fine-grained extrusive rock which is much lighter in colour than basalt, but which is also occasionally found in columns similar to those formed by basalt.

There *are* other igneous rocks to be found in Britain, but if you concentrate your search on the eight we have discussed your chances of locating gemstones will be excellent.

Summary of rocks to look for

Rock	Appearance	Typically seen in
Granite	Coarse-grained; visible crystals; sparkle; light colours—white, grey, pink, yellowish brown	Cornwall, The Lake District, Caernarvonshire, Scotland
Porphyry	As granite, with bands of larger crystals	Westmorland
Gabbro	Coarse-grained; dark green, grey or black	Cornwall, Pembrokeshire, The Lake District, Scotland
Syenite	As granite, but darker in colour; usually grey or reddish hue	Caernarvonshire, Northern Ireland
Diorite	As granite; sometimes dark grey; often mottled green and white	Pembrokeshire
Basalt	Fine-grained; black, dark grey, dark green, dark brown; sometimes seen as columns; sometimes seen as porous scoria	Northern Ireland, Scotland

Dolerite	As basalt, but occurs in sills	Northern England
Andesite	Fine-grained; lighter in colour than basalt, but sometimes seen as columns	Cumberland

4 *Know which rock formations to seek.* At your local lapidary shop you will find many guidebooks for rockhounds which provide long lists of exact locations, mines and quarries recommended for specimens of this or that gemstone. I recommend them to those less adventurous readers prepared to look no further than spots where thousands of rockhounds have looked already. The sites *are* excellent, but they have been very thoroughly searched. Still, you could be lucky!

A far better method of hunting gemstones is to search those areas well off the beaten tracks. It is, of course, more difficult than simply heading for a well-publicized location, but if you teach yourself to recognize the clues which Nature provides, your chances of good finds will be much higher. Just as there are certain igneous rocks you must look out for, so there are certain igneous rock formations you must find if you are to track down those elusive 'crystal flowers'.

Granite outcrops and bosses are the most important of these formations. As we have seen, granite solidified as an intrusive rock beneath the surface of the earth. When the molten magma thrust upwards it often forced the overlying rocks into a huge blister and flowed into the dome thus created. Beneath this protective umbrella the magma was able to cool slowly to form coarse-grained granite which was only exposed when the softer overlying rocks were worn away by weathering. The result is a granite outcrop or boss— hundreds of which are to be found in the wilder regions of Britain. (*See* Fig. 63).

Dykes are masses of igneous rock formed when molten magma was forced upwards between the joints and cracks in the overlying rocks. After the softer material surrounding them has been worn away, the igneous dykes remain as vertical walls of solidified magma which cut across the layers or beds of other rocks. Dykes are widespread in

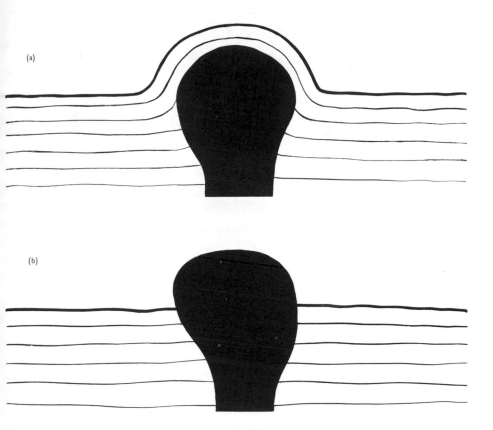

(a)

(b)

igneous regions, and in some places—such as the Isle of Arran—they occur in swarms. On the island of Mull they form rings around large igneous masses (*see* Fig. 64).
Volcanic necks are formed in a similar way. Much of the lava in a volcano is trapped inside the crater. When the volcano dies the lava in the neck hardens to a solid plug which in time weathers to a steep sided hill. A number of these volcanic necks are to be found in Lowland Scotland, notably Arthur's Seat in Edinburgh, and North Berwick Law in East Lothian (*see* Fig. 64).
Sills are formed when molten magma spreads as a horizontal sheet between beds or layers of rock close to the surface. They differ from dykes in that they are parallel to the surrounding beds while dykes are vertical formations. As we have already seen, sills are usually composed of dolerite,

Fig. 63(a) Intrusive magma pushes overlying rocks upwards before it solidifies and (b) when softer overlying rocks are eroded by weathering, the granite is exposed as an outcrop or boss

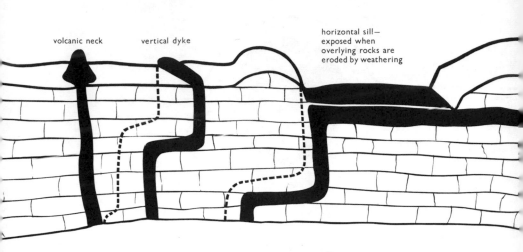

volcanic neck   vertical dyke   horizontal sill—
exposed when
overlying rocks are
eroded by weathering

Fig. 64   and the Great Whin Sill is the best known example in Britain. Remember that sills were formed beneath the earth and exposed by erosion (*see* Fig. 64).

Lava flows can resemble sills in that they sometimes appear as layers between stratified rocks, in spite of the fact that they originally flowed over the surface of the earth. Formed on the surface, they may have been buried later by other rocks and then exposed again by weathering. Their surfaces are sometimes slaggy and cinder-like; or they can have a porous structure caused by bubbles of gas and steam in the original magma; or they can display the typical columnar jointing of basalt. In various parts of Britain, notably North Wales, there are pillow lavas which were formed when volcanic eruptions occurred underwater. As the boiling lava met the cold water its surfaces hardened into pillow-like heaps. Lava flows are common in the igneous regions of Northern Ireland and Scotland (*see* Fig. 65).

5 *Know where the gemstones are found.* So far we have established that the gemstones we are seeking are associated with igneous rocks, including intrusive granites, extrusive basalts and others; and that these rocks are found as outcrops, dykes, sills and lava flows which occur mainly in the mountainous and moorland regions of Britain. Your success at locating

the elusive crystals and veins of semi-precious material which they contain depends, from this point onwards, on how much patience you have and on how well you develop your powers of observation. Even so, we can narrow the search area just a little more by concentrating our efforts on those places within the rock formations where crystals and veins are most likely to be discovered.

Let us assume that you have located an interesting igneous outcrop on some lonely stretch of moorland. This mass of rock might cover anything from a few square yards to many square miles; while the entire outcrop which is visible will only be the exposed area of a far greater mass of solidified magma. You must bear in mind that the igneous rock does not end abruptly where it dips and disappears beneath the surrounding countryside.

We have already seen that igneous rocks are composed of a jumbled mass of tightly cemented crystals—some large, others so small they are invisible to the naked eye. Their size depends on the depth at which the magma cooled, and on how slowly the cooling took place. During this cooling period the gases and steam within the mass escaped, and as they did so they formed bubbles which the hardening magma was unable to close over. The resulting cavity is known as a *druse* and large crystals will often have developed on its walls. Druses can be anything from a few inches to several yards across and they can occur anywhere in the outcrop.

Fig. 65 Typical columnar jointing seen in some basalt lavas

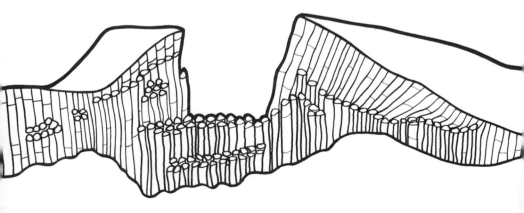

If you find one, use your hammer and chisels very carefully when extracting specimens. Do not attempt to break off single crystals but cut out pieces of the parent rock with crystals attached. This will not only save the crystals from damage, but will also provide you with a much more interesting specimen to display.

Veins are often associated with druses and you should always follow interesting veins across the face of the rock in the hope of finding a druse or a spot where erosion has loosened the material in the veins. Such veins often give the surface of the rock a maggoty appearance.

Pegmatites also occur as veins within the body of the outcrop. They are composed of very large crystals which are often several inches across. Pegmatite veins can also contain druses where extremely large crystals will often have grown.

When the red hot magma thrust its way towards the surface before cooling it often brought with it the molten ores of valuable metals such as tin, lead, silver and gold. When the ores cooled they formed *lodes*, and it is these which miners seek when they sink shafts into the rock. Lodes are always bordered by what are known as *gangue minerals* which include quartz, tourmaline, topaz, fluorite and many more of the semi-precious gemstones you are hoping to find. Remembering that the miner is after the ores in the lode, it will be obvious that if your particular outcrop has a disused mine on or near it, the *spoil heap* is the 'hot spot' you should head for because that is where the miner will have thrown the gangue, or waste.

The best spoil heaps are those much overgrown with weeds; they are better still if they are well off the beaten track. You could be the first gem hunter to pick them over since the long departed miners dumped them. Locate the most inaccessible part of the heap—perhaps hidden under bushes—and dig in, keeping your eyes peeled for the attractive colour, sparkle or shape of crystals.

You may, of course, find very small lodes which have not been worked by miners because the ores occur in only tiny, uneconomical quantities. Many attractive specimens can be chiselled out of these minor lodes, where you should also look out for cavities in the gangue, similar to the druses mentioned above, where beautiful crystals can develop.

The perimeters of igneous outcrops are also very likely to contain gemstones. The tremendous heat from the magma baked and changed the surrounding rocks which it touched—a process which geologists call *contact metamorphism*. This baked area around the igneous rock is known as the *aureole* or *halo* and it can measure anything from a few inches to a mile or more in width, depending on the size of the igneous mass and the heat which the molten magma generated. The surrounding rocks are changed in character and often they have been melted and have resolidified to produce entirely new minerals and sometimes large and interesting crystals (*see* Fig. 66).

One of the ways in which a lava flow differs from a sill is in the nature of its baked zone. Contact metamorphism will have occurred above and below a sill because it was formed as a layer *between* the surrounding rocks. A lava flow, on the other hand, will have altered only those rocks which lie immediately beneath it because it originally flowed across the *surface* of the earth. In lava flows the likely places to find gem material—in addition to the baked zone—are the cavities formed when gas and steam bubbled out of the molten material. Because the lava was flowing when they

Fig. 66

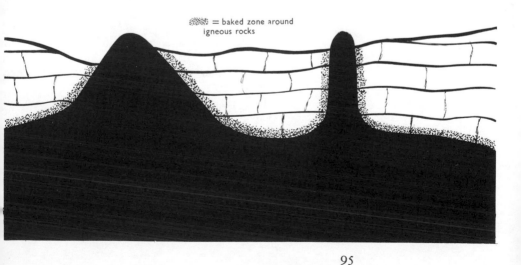

= baked zone around igneous rocks

were formed, these cavities are often stretched or almond-shaped. They óften contain agate or chalcedony, and they are known to geologists as *amygdales*.

If the area you are searching is close to a *stream*—a very common occurrence in mountainous regions—the stream bed is well worth searching for gem material in the shape of fragments torn from the rocks by the erosive power of the rushing water. Readers of my book, *Bottle Collecting*, will find the glass-bottomed buckets and plastic tubes described in that book ideal when searching mountain streams for semi-precious gems.

Finally, you must always be on the look out for *quarries*, *railway cuttings* and *road works* in any area close to igneous rock formations. Inaccessible veins, lodes and druses are often exposed when cuttings are made for roads or railways; while in quarries, which are often found in igneous regions because such rocks are used for road-making, new material is constantly being exposed. It is essential that permission to search such places—particularly working quarries—is obtained *before* you start your search. A polite request will only rarely meet with a refusal.

Summary of likely gemstone haunts in igneous rocks

Druses	Cavities caused by gases or steam in cooling magma of intrusive rocks.
Veins	Bands of crystals running across the face of the outcrop.
Pegmatites	Igneous rock made up of very large crystals; contains druses and veins.
Lodes	Bodies of ore.
Gangue	The material surrounding a lode; often contains excellent gemstones.
Spoil heap	The spot near a mine where the gangue has been dumped.
Aureole	The baked area immediately surrounding an igneous body of rock.
Amygdales	Cavities formed by gases or steam in extrusive lava flows.
Stream beds	Wherever they cut through igneous rocks.
Quarries and cuttings	In igneous regions.

Further study

This very brief look we have taken at igneous rocks and their modes of occurrence should guide you to some interesting finds. I hope that it will also stimulate a lasting interest in geology, and that you will go on from this very sketchy introduction to a scientific study of the subject. If you do, many more exciting gems await you. I have confined the 'geology' in this chapter to igneous rocks because they are fairly easy to find, and because they will introduce you to some beautiful scenery. Please do not imagine that I have exhausted the subject of gemstone locations. Nothing could be further from the truth. I have not mentioned regional metamorphism, gneiss, schists, geodes, marcasite nodules, and the many other subjects which a detailed study of geology will bring to your attention. With greater knowledge you will be able to spread your gem-hunting net even wider and greatly improve your chances of excellent finds. The more you know, the better will be your finds; the better your finds, the more you will want to know.

The gemstones you might find

Positive identification of your gemstones is not terribly important during your early days as a rockhound. Concentrate on finding them, noting their locations on your maps, and, whenever possible, extracting your specimens attached to samples of the surrounding rock. If you then take your finds to a rock shop, local museum or lapidary club you are sure to find someone able to tell you exactly what you have found.

Many rock shops have expert staff who are always delighted to help beginners identify their finds. At some shops, particularly those close to the area you have been searching, you will be able to buy small samples of local gemstones. They are usually attractively boxed, have neat identification labels attached, are quite modestly priced, and well worth buying if you intend to do most of your gem hunting in that particular area.

You will find large specimens of local rocks and minerals on display in many museums, and an afternoon spent browsing in a museum is time well spent. My first find as a rockhound was a small cluster of cubic crystals with a violet tint which I picked up on the spoil heap of an abandoned mine in County Durham. At the time I had no idea what I had found. The crystals were beautiful and I had found them; that was all that mattered. Months later, while browsing in Middlesbrough Museum, I spotted an identical specimen in a display cabinet and eagerly read the printed card beneath. To my delight I learned that I had in fact found a cluster of fluorite crystals. You may find it easier to wait until you find something you cannot identify and then take it to a museum in the hope of spotting a similar specimen rather than read up and memorize facts about gems you may never find before you start looking. In this way you will add to your knowledge slowly but surely.

Joining a local lapidary club is a good idea even if you do not intend to cut and polish gemstones. You will meet many other enthusiasts who will be able to answer any questions you have about rocks, minerals and gemstones. Every member started as an absolute beginner like you and you will find them very sympathetic listeners. Many clubs organize rockhounding excursions to a wide variety of collecting areas, and by joining in you will add to your knowledge and to your collection.

The following brief notes on possible finds in igneous regions will start you on the road to gemstone identification. When you make a find check the notes to see if you can decide what it is you have found. If you cannot do so, put it in your rucksack and look it up when you get home.

Agate	Formed when silica solutions filled gas and steam cavities (amygdales) in cooling lavas. When cut, reveals coloured banding caused by various minerals in the original solution. Often almond-shaped. They weather out of the surrounding rock and are often found on beaches and in mountain streams. Colours: bands including white, black, yellow and blue. Good locations: beaches of Scotland and Northern Ireland.
Amethyst	Formed when silica crystallized out of molten magma. Usually found in granite where large crystals can develop in vein cavities (druses). Colours: shades of purple common, green and others not unknown. Good locations: Cornish granites.
Andalusite	Can be found in metamorphic aurcoles. Crystals are

	usually thick cubes coated with sparkling mica flakes. Colours: greyish pink, dark green, brown, yellow, red. Good locations: Durham, Cumberland.
Apatite	Usually found in gangues bordering ore-bearing lodes (especially tin) in granite. Also occurs in gabbro. Colours: crystals are usually green, but can be blue, brick red, yellow or colourless. Good locations: spoil heaps of abandoned tin mines in Cornwall.
Azurite	A blue carbonate of copper usually found encrusted to rocks and minerals in a 'cluster of grapes' (botryoidal) formation. Occasionally as thick, plate-like crystals in gangues bordering ore-bearing lodes (especially copper) in granite. Colour: azure blue. Good locations: spoil heaps of abandoned copper mines in north Lancashire, Cumberland, Cheshire, North Wales and Cornwall.
Beryl	Usually found as veins in granite where large crystals might develop in druses. Crystals are usually pencil-like (hexagonal). Colours: green, blue, yellow. Good locations: Cairngorm Mountains, Mourne Mountains, Devon, Cornwall, Arran.
Cairngorm	As amethyst. Colour: smoky brown. Good locations: Cairngorm Mountains.
Calcite	Usually found in gangues bordering ore bearing lodes. Crystals range widely in shape. Will effervesce when a small drop of vinegar is placed on the specimen. Colours: white, colourless, often with tints on crystal tips. Good locations: Cornwall, Merionethshire, north Yorkshire.
Cassiterite	Tin oxide; found in gangues bordering ore-bearing lodes (especially tin) in granite. Often found in association with apatite. Crystals range widely in shape. Colours: reddish brown to black. Good locations: spoil heaps of abandoned tin mines in Cornwall.
Chalcedony	As agate. Colours: greyish blue. Good locations: Cumberland, Perthshire.
Citrine	As amethyst. Colours: shades of yellow. Good locations: Cornwall.
Cornelian	As agate. Colours: red. Good locations: Cumberland, Arran.
Epidote	Found widely in igneous formations, but good specimens uncommon. Crystals are elongated pencil shapes,

	easily confused with tourmaline. Colours: a wide range including dark green, bluish green, brown, yellow. Good locations: Cornwall, Merionethshire.
Fluorite	Found widely in igneous formations, but best locations are gangues bordering ore-bearing lodes (especially lead, zinc and copper); and in metamorphic aureoles. The crystals are usually cubes. Colours: a wide range including violet, green, yellow and blue. Good locations: Durham, Cumberland, Derbyshire.
Garnet	Can be found in metamorphic aureoles and granite outcrops. Crystals are usually multi-sided and are found singly embedded in the parent rock. Colours: although red is best known colour, garnets are often brown, green or yellow. Good locations: Northern Scotland, Westmorland, Devon, Fifeshire.
Haematite	Also known as 'Kidney Ore' because it often occurs as kidney-shaped masses; usually in gangues bordering ore bearing lodes, though it is fairly widespread in igneous regions. Colours: reddish brown. Good locations: Cumberland.
Jasper	As agate. An admixture of clayey material in the silica solution produces jasper. Colours: red, green and variations of red and green. When the green variety is spotted with red dots it is known as bloodstone. Good locations: Most beaches of Scotland, Northern Ireland and North Wales.
Labradorite	Can be found in basalts. It often shimmers with a play of colours not unlike opal. Colours: various, including green, pale blue, yellow. Good locations: Antrim, Derbyshire.
Malachite	As azurite, but a green carbonate of copper. Colours: light to a blackish green. Good locations: spoil heaps of abandoned copper mines in Cumberland, Cheshire, Lanarkshire, Cornwall, North Wales, Durham and Derbyshire.
Natrolite	Found in basalts as pyramid-topped, elongated cubes. Colours: white, yellow, or pink, with a satin sheen. Good locations: Northern Ireland, Staffordshire, Renfrewshire.
Olivine	Usually found in basalts and volcanic necks. Colours: olive green, bright green, brown. Good locations: Derbyshire, West Lothian, Antrim.
Opal	Opal is a mixture of silica and water and is commonly found in basalts and lavas where it occurs in amygdales. Colours: a milky sheen with a play of rainbow colours.

	Good locations: Antrim, Tyrone, Argyllshire, Devon.
Prehnite	Found in basalt and in lava amygdales, often in 'cluster of grapes' (botryoidal) formations; occasionally as flat, tablet-like crystals. Colours: green, yellow, white.
	Good locations: Northern Ireland, Ayrshire, Skye.
Rhodonite	A silicate of manganese found in gangues bordering ore-bearing lodes (especially lead and zinc) in granite. Usually occurs in tight veins, Crystals are rare. Colours: pink and red with a pearly lustre and, often, with wavy banding of lighter and darker shades.
	Good locations: Devon, Cornwall, Lanarkshire.
Sphene	Found as wedge-shaped and tabular crystals in granite and diorite. Colours: yellow, green, brown, black—all with characteristic lustre and fire.
	Good locations: Pembrokeshire, Morayshire.
Spinel	Can be found in metamorphic aureoles around intrusive igneous rocks. Colours: blue, red, brown.
	Good locations: Sutherland, Antrim.
Topaz	Found in granite, and as a gangue mineral in ore-bearing lodes (especially tin). Crystals have a multisided, flat-topped pyramid shape.
	Good locations: Cairngorm Mountains, Cornwall, Lewis.
Tourmaline	Found in granite and in metamorphic aureoles. Crystals are usually long prisms showing lengthwise grooves. Colours: glassy black, brown, dark green, dark blue, red.
	Good locations: Cornwall, Devon, Sutherland, Perthshire.
Zircon	Found in granite. Colours: red, colourless, green, pale yellow—all with characteristic lustre and fire.
	Good locations: Sutherland, Argyllshire, Fifeshire.

Fig. 67 The Cairngorm mountains, Scotland, where many rocks and gems can be found

9 Buying stones and fittings

Rough rock is the raw material of lapidary. Without adequate and inexpensive supplies the hobby would be beyond the reach of the vast majority of people unable to visit those exotic lands where semi-precious stones are commonplace. The agate nodule you casually cast your eyes over when browsing through the stocks at your local rock shop may not look very special, yet it was probably hacked out of its parent rock by a dusky labourer toiling in a mine somewhere in South America. On its journey to the rock shop in your High Street it was probably carried over narrow mountain roads, jungle tracks and deep oceans; it passed through loading bays, railway sidings, distribution depots and wholesale warehouses; its size, colour and weight were recorded with those of other specimens by mine foremen, shipping agents, sea captains, port officials, merchants, exporters, importers, wholesalers and finally by your rock shop manager in his mail order catalogue. Thus a substantial industry has grown up to meet the raw material demands of amateur lapidaries.

If you own a slab saw you can reduce the costs of your rough rock quite considerably by buying large, unslabbed pieces. One of the many benefits of joining your local lapidary club is that you will probably be able to use an even larger saw owned by the club to cut pieces too bulky for your equipment. You may also find that the club places large orders with rock importers on behalf of all members who benefit from a wholesale discount.

Those who prefer to enjoy the hobby in solitude need not despair. There are a number of ways in which you can track down excellent bargains when buying your stocks. The first is to buy from a dealer who handles good quality material. Rough rock is graded into first and second qualities and though second quality material often sounds like a bargain I advise you to buy only top grade material if you wish to avoid disappointing results.

When making your purchases by mail order it is a good plan to write to several suppliers and compare catalogues and price lists. The least expensive rock is unlikely to be the best, but there are quite wide price variations between dealers. Initially you should buy very small quantities from a number of dealers and compare the qualities of each consignment. Once you have found a dealer whose material is good you should stick to him. Such loyalty is beneficial to both parties; with regular customers the dealer can place larger orders with his suppliers and pass on to you some of the saving *and* some of the better quality material he obtains by doing this. In addition he will probably keep you informed about any small lots of special material he obtains which do not appear in his regular catalogue.

The range of material you can buy from mail order rock and mineral dealers is sufficiently wide to keep you cutting, grinding, and polishing for a lifetime. The list given below was compiled from the catalogues of a dozen British suppliers and it is by no means exhaustive. Only those rocks which appeared in at least three catalogues have been included and most dealers you approach will have an even wider selection. The descriptions of the fifty-odd specimens listed here were also taken from dealers' catalogues and they show that almost half of the rocks listed are available from at least two world sources—another reason why you should shop around before buying large quantities.

Selection of imported rough rock available from British dealers

Agate	Brazilian beans in red, blue and white; Australian nodules with green and red banding; South African stalactite; Brazilian nodules with cornelian; Botswana pink; Brazilian nodules with brown, blue and grey banding; Indian zebra with white and black banding; South African water-worn pebbles; Mexican tree with black and white markings; Indian tree with green and white markings; Mexican crazy lace; Moroccan banded white and grey; Indian black; African plume with yellow and green banding; South African blue lace; Indian moss.
Amber	East German pale yellow.
Amethyst	South African phantom with white and purple zig-zag banding; Mexican deep purple; Brazilian purple; Russian pale.
Amazonite	American pale turquoise; Canadian blue green; Norwegian pale blue; South African green with white and brown streaks.
Apatite	Mexican lemon.

Aquamarine	Mexican sea blue.
Aragonite	South African pale yellow with white banding.
Aventurine	Brazilian deep green; Indian blue.
Azurite	Congolese deep blue.
Bloodstone	Indian dark green well spotted with red; Indian mottled green, red and purple.
Cairngorm	Brazilian deep brown.
Chalcedony	Brazilian in two shades of green.
Chrysoprase	American bright green; Brazilian pale; Australian deep green nodules.
Citrine	Brazilian pale yellow.
Coral	Australian black; Mediterranean red.
Cornelian	Indian orange; South American red.
Cricolite	Mexican with grey, blue and green swirls.
Epidote	North American apple green.
Fossil wood	Canadian grey, brown, pink and red; American rainbow; Australian chinchilla.
Garnet	Indian almandine in deep burgundy; South African grossular in yellow; Tanzanian almandine in dark red; Rhodesian pyrope in crimson; Russian andradite in green.
Hickorite	Mexican with red, yellow, brown and purple bands, North American light tan and brick red.
Jasper	Indian red; Indian brown and green; South African deep red; Australian cream and orange.
Kunzite	North American pink.
Kyanite	North American deep aquamarine.
Labradorite	North American green, yellow, blue and red.
Lapis lazuli	Russian ultramarine; South African blue streaked with white; Afghanistan royal blue.
Malachite	Congolese deep green; Russian pale blue.
Marble	Argentinian onyx; Peruvian onyx; Connemara green and white; Iona in shades of green.
Moonstone	Indian white.
Nephrite jade	Canadian deep green.
Obsidian	American snowflake; American black sheen.
Olivine	North American deep green.
Opal	Italian white; Australian fire.
Opalite	Australian with yellow fern patterns.
Peridote	North American deep green.
Petalite	African pink.
Prehnite	Australian green and yellow.
Pyrite	Spanish golden.
Rhodochrosite	Argentinian pale satin pink.
Rhodonite	Argentinian deep red and black; Australian pink and black.

Ribbonstone	Australian with multi-coloured stripes.
Rose quartz	Brazilian cloudy pink; South African pink.
Rutilated quartz	Brazilian clear with golden needles.
Serpentine	Mexican lemon green; Norwegian deep green; Botswana lime green.
Sodalite	South African dark blue; Indian deep blue.
Spodumene	North American light green.
Sunstone	Norwegian pink and orange; Indian golden.
Tiger eye	South African yellow; South African red; South African blue.
Thulite	Norwegian pink and green.
Topaz	Brazilian yellow; Brazilian blue; Nigerian water-worn pebbles in light blue and brown.
Tourmaline	Brazilian dark green; Brazilian red; Brazilian green and blue.
Verdite	South African pale green
Wollestonite	Mexican pale yellow.
Zircon	Australian clear, orange and red.

Fittings

The range of fittings available to the home jewellery-maker compares very favourably with the range of rough rock. You should have no difficulty in locating your particular requirements if you shop around and study the catalogues of as many suppliers as possible. No two dealers offer identical fittings and you may find that you have to buy from several suppliers in order to obtain those you need. Placing several small orders in this way can be uneconomical; if possible you should order supplies to last several months at one time as this will mean that you qualify for the small discount usually given on bulk orders. You may find that your local lapidary club has bulk buying arrangements with several suppliers.

Fittings are made in a number of metals and finishes—stainless steel, Sterling silver, 9 carat gold, copper, silver- and gold-plated, and yellow or white metal. To avoid delays in dealing with your order you should always check that the catalogue from which you are ordering lists a particular fitting in the metal or finish you require, and make sure that you state your exact requirements on the order sheet. Most suppliers offer a return post service for mail order customers, but delays are inevitable if vital information is missing from the order.

Rings	Most have adjustable shanks (open or split), though the more expensive silver and gold varieties are available with solid shanks. Dealers selling rings with solid shanks usually supply a ring size card free of charge. Rings for cabochons will always have cabochon sizes clearly stated in the catalogue. Plain, lace and claw settings are made.
Ear fittings	Available as clips, screws and wires. Always sold in pairs. Some have a flat plate to take a calibrated cabochon.
Brooches	A wide variety available including fobs, bars, leaves, circles, rings and button-backs. Some have safety catches. Often available in copper and stainless steel.
Bracelets	Available with flat pads, cabochon fittings or as a simple chain to which charms can be attached.
Key rings	Available with mesh or snake chain. Some have safety catches.
Cuff links	Usually of the spring lever type. Available with flat pads or cabochon fittings. Always sold in pairs.
Tie fittings	These include crocodile clips, tie tacks and pins.
Chain	Available in many thicknesses and styles. It is more economical to buy chain by the yard and fit your own bolt rings which can be bought separately when making pendants and necklaces.
Cast mounts	These are sold in a wide range of designs includ-flower sprays, human figures, animals, crosses and geometric shapes. A range of Celtic designs is also available in an antique silver finish.
Fittings for polished slabs and specimens	Ballpoint pens with holders which are screwed or cemented to the slab; perpetual calendars; metal stands for polished specimens.

Many dealers also sell packaging material for finished jewellery. These include hinged-lid boxes for rings, ear fittings and cufflinks, plastic boxes for brooches and leather-covered boxes for bracelets and pendants.

The following list of shops, clubs and other addresses of interest to lapidary enthusiasts is as comprehensive as was possible at the time of writing. Rock shops are now opening in most towns in Britain and lapidary and rockhounding clubs are being formed almost as quickly whenever a dozen or so enthusiasts get together. An excellent source of information about new shops and clubs is *Gems*, the monthly British Lapidary Magazine (see address on p. 110) which you should read regularly for up-to-date information on lapidary activities in your area.

It would be difficult to give complete details about the range of machinery, gemstones and fittings offered by every rock shop on this list, but if you write to the addresses given and enclose a stamped addressed envelope you will receive comprehensive catalogues which will enable you to order your requirements by mail. Many of the shops are exciting places to visit, where you will be able to see the machines covered in this book and obtain friendly advice on any aspect of lapidary. To give you an idea of what you can expect on your first visit to a rock shop here are brief descriptions of four establishments I visited recently. A similar range of machines, rough rock, fittings, books and other accessories should be available at the shop of your choice.

Gemrocks Ltd. An 'Aladdin's Cave' situated in the centre of London. Enormous range of British, American and Australian machines including trim saws, slab saws, laps, grinders and combination units. A beautiful display of polished slabs always on show; wide range of rough rock, books and fittings.

M. L. Beach Ltd. A fascinating shop which, to quote from their literature, specializes in 'unusual leisure items for thinking people'. The company manufactures a range of lapidary equipment and 'Beach' tumblers and horizontal combination units have a world-wide reputation. Browsers are more than welcome and the variety of rough rock should keep you happy all day.

Kernowcraft Ltd. If you are on holiday in Cornwall this

shop is a perfect place to spend a rainy afternoon. British and Australian machines are stocked and there is a good selection of polished slabs, rough rock, books and fittings.

Ammonite Ltd.   Worth a visit whenever you are in South Wales. A wide range of imported machines including large slab saws, trim saws, combination units, faceting machines and tumblers. Fittings, tools and books are also stocked. There is an interesting display of collector's specimens and Ammonite's well-known range of fossil replicates. School parties are especially welcome.

Other suppliers   Kernowcraft Rocks & Gems Ltd, 44 Lemon Street, Truro, Cornwall

The Gem Rock and Lapidary Centre, 41 Fore Street, St. Just, Penzance, Cornwall

H. & T. Gems, 31 Rosebury Road, Hartlepool, Co. Durham

Hirsh Jacobson, 91 Marylebone High Street, London, W.1

M. L. Beach (Products) Ltd, 41 Church Street, Twickenham, Middlesex

Fig. 68   The interior of a lapidary shop

Portbeag Pebblecraft, Albany Street, Oban, Scotland
Fidra Stone Shop, 47 Meeting House Lane, Brighton, Sussex
Tideswell Dale Rockshop, Tideswell, Derbyshire
The Jam Pot, Slaidburn, Clitheroe, Lancashire
Tumble Kraft, 10 High Street, Rochester, Kent
Caverswall Minerals, The Dams, Caverswall, Stoke-on-Trent, Staffordshire
A. & D. Hughes Ltd, Popes Lane, Oldbury, Warley, Worcestershire
Baines Orr Ltd, 1–5 Garlands Road, Redhill, Surrey
Howard Minerals Ltd, 27 Heddon Street, London, W.1
Rocks, Gems, and Crafts Centre, 494 Nottingham Road, Chaddesden, Derby
A. Massie & Son, 158 Burgoyne Road, Sheffield, 6, Yorkshire
Solent Lapidary, 145 Highland Road, Southsea, Hampshire
Fife Stone Craft, 3 Edison House, Fullerton Road, Glenrothes, Fife.
Norgems, 4 Front Street, Sandbach, Cheshire
Whithear Lapidary Co, 35 Ballards Lane, London, N.3
Ammonite Ltd, Llandow, Cowbridge, Glamorgan, CF7 7PB.
Scotrocks Partners, 48 Park Road, Glasgow, C.4
Stones & Settings, 54 Main Street, Prestwick, Scotland
Avon Gems, Strathavon, Boon Street, Eckington, Pershore, Worcestershire
Geobright, 28 Queens Road, Brighton, Sussex
Hillside Gems, Wylde Green, Sutton Coldfield, Warwickshire
PMR Lapidary Equipment, Pitlochry, Perthshire
Marbleshop, Portsoy, Banff, Scotland
Timgems, The Old Shop, Ludham, Great Yarmouth, Norfolk
Glenjoy Lapidary Supplies, 89 Westgate, Wakefield, Yorkshire, WF1 1EL
Rough & Tumble Ltd, 3 Tyne Street, North Shields, Northumberland.
The Rockhound Shop, Newbiggin, Northumberland
Tudor Amethyst, 24 West Street, Exeter, Devon
Gemstones, 44 Walmsley Street, Hull, Yorkshire
Craftorama, 14 Endell Street, London, W.C.2
C. & N. Mineral Supplies, Adelphi Chambers, Shakespeare Street, Newcastle-on-Tyne, Northumberland
Lakeland Rock Shop, Packhorse Yard, Main Street, Keswick, Cumberland
Gemrocks Ltd, 20/30 Holborn, London, E.C.1

Key Minerals, Brienz, Hendra Road, St. Dennis, St. Austell, Cornwall

Gemset of Broadstairs Ltd, 31 Albion Street, Broadstairs, Kent

Harrisons, 174 Woodlands Road, Glasgow, C.3

Gemlines, 10 Victoria Crescent, London, S.W.19

C. Kilpatrick, 27 Colsea Road, Cove Bay, Aberdeen

Gemlode, 35 Bolton Road, Chessington, Surrey

Tor Minerals, 2 The Orchard, Trevanson, Wadebridge, Cornwall.

Doreen Jewellery Mounts, 49 Elizabeth Road, Brentwood, Essex

Keystones, 1 Local Board Road, Watford, Hertfordshire

Opie Gems, 13 Gilbert Close, Hempstead, Gillingham, Kent

Love-Rocks, 56/58 North Street, Bedminster, Bristol

Rocks and Minerals, 4 Moorcourt Drive, Cheltenham, Gloucester

The Stone Corner, 21 High Street, Hastings, Sussex

Merritt, Eastleigh Road, Devizes, Wiltshire

Jacinth Gems, 10 Highfield Crescent, Southampton, Hampshire

D. M. Minerals, 18a Cathcart Street, Ayr

Mineral Imports, 72 Netheravon Road, London, W4 2NB

Natural Gems Ltd, Kingsbury Square, Aylesbury, Buckinghamshire

Pebblegem, 88a Wallis Road, London, E9 5LN

Quercus Gems, Lindisfarne House, Rucklers Lane, Kings Langley, Hertfordshire

Little Rocks, 36 Oakwood Avenue, Cardiff, Glamorgan

R. Lane, 'The Haven', Danes Road, Awbridge, Romsey, Hampshire

Worldwide Mineralogical Co., Great Shelford, Cambridge

W. A. Bolton, 19 Lynwood Road, Liverpool, 9

J. L. Newbigin, 13 Narrowgate, Alnwick, Northumberland

Magazines *Gems*, 29 Ludgate Hill, London, E.C.4
Rockhound, 24–9 Trellick Tower, 5 Golborne Road, London, W.10
Lapidary Journal, P.O. Box 80937–E, San Diego, California, 92138, U.S.A.

Clubs Pentland Lapidary Society, 12 Kirkgate, Currie, Midlothian
Sutherland Rockhounds, Lonemore, Dornoch, Sutherland
Scottish Mineral & Lapidary Club, 22b St. Giles Street, Edinburgh, 1

West of Scotland Mineral & Lapidary Society, 82 Dumbreck Road, Glasgow, S.1.

Borders Lapidary Club, 47 Albert Place, Galashiels, Selkirkshire

Kingston Lapidary Society, 219 Summergangs Road, Hull, Yorkshire

Danum Lapidary Society, 39 St. Augustines Road, Bessacarr, Doncaster, Yorkshire

Teesside Lapidary Society, 65 Staindrop Drive, Acklam, Middlesbrough, Teesside

Whitehaven Lapidary Society, 110 Tomlin Avenue, Mirehouse, Whitehaven, Cumberland

Harrogate Lapidary Society, 71 Wetherby Road, Harrogate, Yorkshire

Leeds Lapidary Society, 2 Earlswood Avenue, Leeds LS8 2BR

Warrington Lapidary Society, 28 Thelwall New Road, Thelwall, Warrington, Lancashire

Stanley Rockhound Club, 24 Cecil Street, East Stanley, Co. Durham

Huddersfield Mineralogical Society, 25 Branch Street, Paddock, Huddersfield, Yorkshire

Peak District Rock & Mineral Society, Youth Centre, Tideswell, Derby

Sheffield Amateur Geological Society, 5 Hutcliffe Wood Road, Sheffield, Yorkshire

North West Lapidary Society, 79 Dean Drive, Wilmslow, Cheshire

Cheltenham Mineral Society, 2 Westcote Road, Tuffley, Gloucester

West Midlands Lapidary Society, 148 Foleshill Road, Coventry, Warwickshire

Cambridge Lapidary Club, 93 Queen Edith's Way, Cambridge

Amateur Geological Society, Hampstead Garden Suburb Institute, Central Square, London, N.W.11

Essex Rock & Mineral Society, 176 Wanstead Park Road, Ilford, Essex

North Surrey Lapidary Society, 28 The Causeway, Carshalton, Surrey

West Surrey Lapidary Society, 10 Whitemore Green, Hale, Farnham, Surrey

Dartford Lapidary Society, 45a Elmdene Road, London, S.E.18.

Thanet Mineral Society, 5 Maisons Rise, Broadstairs, Kent

Wessex Lapidary Society, 1 Avenue Road, Winchester, Hampshire

Bristol Lapidary Society, 10 Grove Park, Redland, Bristol
Bath Lapidary Society, 10 Pulteney Street, Bath
Southampton Lapidary Society, 52 Kinross Road, Totton
Southampton
Plymouth Mineral and Mining Club, 36 Ponsonby Road, Mile
house, Plymouth, Devon
Mid-Cornwall Rocks and Minerals Club, 91 Queens Crescent
Bodmin, Cornwall
Dorset Mineral Club, 70 Manor Road, Dorchester, Dorset
Irish Lapidary Society, Grafton Court, Grafton Street, Dublin,

Maps showing the location of rocks and gems in Britain

In the following pages I have given some likely gemstone haunts in the British Isles. No rockhounding maps have been included for those areas (eastern and south-eastern England) which are not rich in precious or semi-precious stones.

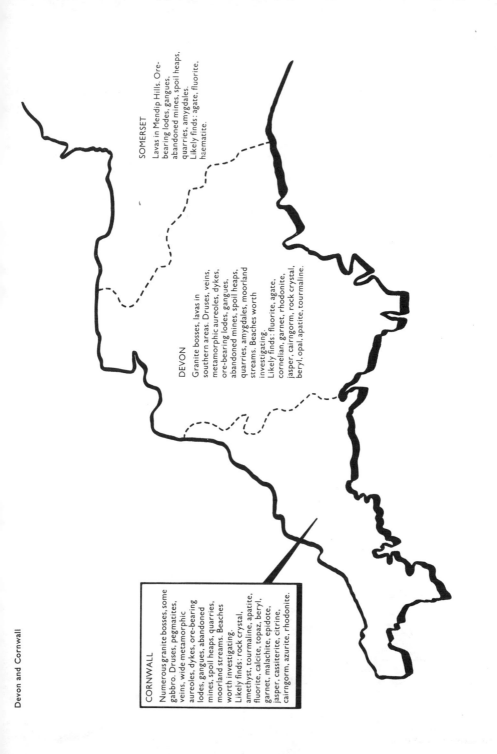

Devon and Cornwall

SOMERSET

Lavas in Mendip Hills. Ore-bearing lodes, gangues, abandoned mines, spoil heaps, quarries, amygdales.
Likely finds: agate, fluorite, haematite.

DEVON

Granite bosses, lavas in southern areas. Druses, veins, metamorphic aureoles, dykes, ore-bearing lodes, gangues, abandoned mines, spoil heaps, quarries, amygdales, moorland streams. Beaches worth investigating.
Likely finds: fluorite, agate, cornelian, garnet, rhodonite, jasper, cairngorm, rock crystal, beryl, opal, apatite, tourmaline.

CORNWALL

Numerous granite bosses, some gabbro. Druses, pegmatites, veins, wide metamorphic aureoles, dykes, ore-bearing lodes, gangues, abandoned mines, spoil heaps, quarries, moorland streams. Beaches worth investigating.
Likely finds: rock crystal, amethyst, tourmaline, apatite, fluorite, calcite, topaz, beryl, garnet, malachite, epidote, jasper, cassiterite, citrine, cairngorm, azurite, rhodonite.

Wales

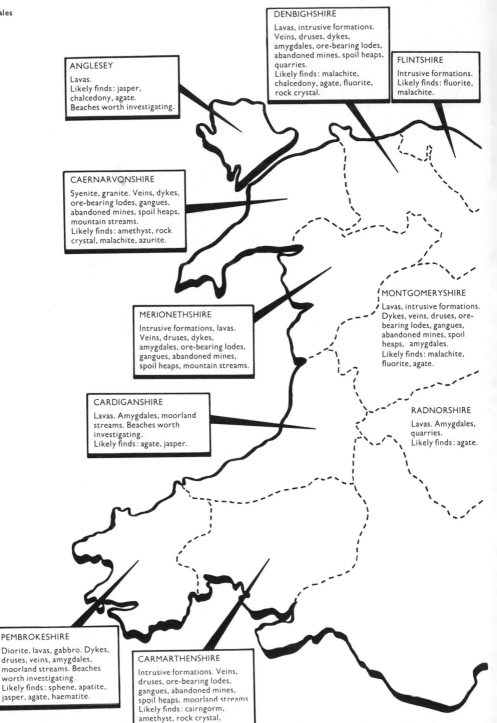

ANGLESEY

Lavas.
Likely finds: jasper,
chalcedony, agate.
Beaches worth investigating.

DENBIGHSHIRE

Lavas, intrusive formations.
Veins, druses, dykes,
amygdales, ore-bearing lodes,
abandoned mines, spoil heaps,
quarries.
Likely finds: malachite,
chalcedony, agate, fluorite,
rock crystal.

FLINTSHIRE

Intrusive formations.
Likely finds: fluorite,
malachite.

CAERNARVONSHIRE

Syenite, granite. Veins, dykes,
ore-bearing lodes, gangues,
abandoned mines, spoil heaps,
mountain streams.
Likely finds: amethyst, rock
crystal, malachite, azurite.

MERIONETHSHIRE

Intrusive formations, lavas.
Veins, druses, dykes,
amygdales, ore-bearing lodes,
gangues, abandoned mines,
spoil heaps, mountain streams.

MONTGOMERYSHIRE

Lavas, intrusive formations.
Dykes, veins, druses, ore-
bearing lodes, gangues,
abandoned mines, spoil
heaps, amygdales.
Likely finds: malachite,
fluorite, agate.

CARDIGANSHIRE

Lavas. Amygdales, moorland
streams. Beaches worth
investigating.
Likely finds: agate, jasper.

RADNORSHIRE

Lavas. Amygdales,
quarries.
Likely finds: agate.

PEMBROKESHIRE

Diorite, lavas, gabbro. Dykes,
druses, veins, amygdales,
moorland streams. Beaches
worth investigating.
Likely finds: sphene, apatite,
jasper, agate, haematite.

CARMARTHENSHIRE

Intrusive formations. Veins,
druses, ore-bearing lodes,
gangues, abandoned mines,
spoil heaps, moorland streams
Likely finds: cairngorm,
amethyst, rock crystal,
haematite.

CUMBERLAND

Lavas, granite, andesite.
Metamorphic aureoles, veins,
druses, dykes, ore-bearing
lodes, gangues, abandoned
mines, spoil heaps, mountain
streams, quarries, amygdales.
Beaches worth investigating.
Likely finds: agate, cornelian,
jasper, chalcedony, cairngorm,
rock crystal, tourmaline,
andalusite, malachite,
apatite, fluorite, haematite,
azurite, calcite.

NORTHUMBERLAND

Granite, lavas, dolerite. Dykes,
sills, veins, druses, amygdales,
ore-bearing lodes, abandoned
mines, spoil heaps, quarries,
moorland streams.
Likely finds: rock crystal,
fluorite, amethyst, agate.

DURHAM

Dolerite. Sills, metamorphic
aureoles, dykes, veins, ore-
bearing lodes, abandoned
mines, spoil heaps, quarries,
moorland streams.
Likely finds: fluorite, rock
crystal, andalusite, garnet,
malachite.

WESTMORLAND

Granite, porphyry, pegmatites.
Veins, druses, metamorphic
aureoles, ore-bearing lodes,
gangues, abandoned mines,
spoil heaps, mountain streams,
quarries.
Likely finds: garnet, cairngorm,
fluorite.

YORKSHIRE

Intrusive formations in north.
Veins, druses, ore-bearing
lodes, gangues, abandoned
mines, spoil heaps, moorland
streams.
Likely finds: fluorite, calcite.

DERBYSHIRE

Intrusive formations, lavas,
basalt. Druses, veins, ore-
bearing lodes, abandoned
mines, spoil heaps, quarries,
moorland streams, amygdales.
Likely finds: fluorite, rock
crystal, amethyst, cairngorm,
chalcedony, agate, olivine,
malachite, haematite, opal,
labradorite.

LANCASHIRE

Gabbro and granite in north.
Veins, druses, ore-bearing
lodes, gangues, abandoned
mines, spoil heaps, quarries,
moorland streams.
Likely finds: rock crystal,
fluorite, haematite.

CHESHIRE

Intrusive formations. Veins,
druses, ore-bearing lodes,
gangues, abandoned mines,
spoil heaps.
Likely finds: malachite, azurite.

SHROPSHIRE

Intrusive formations. Veins,
druses, ore-bearing lodes,
gangues, abandoned mines,
spoil heaps, quarries.
Likely finds: rock crystal,
fluorite, malachite.

STAFFORDSHIRE

Basalt. Dykes, veins, druses.
Likely finds: olivine, natrolite.

Southern Scotland

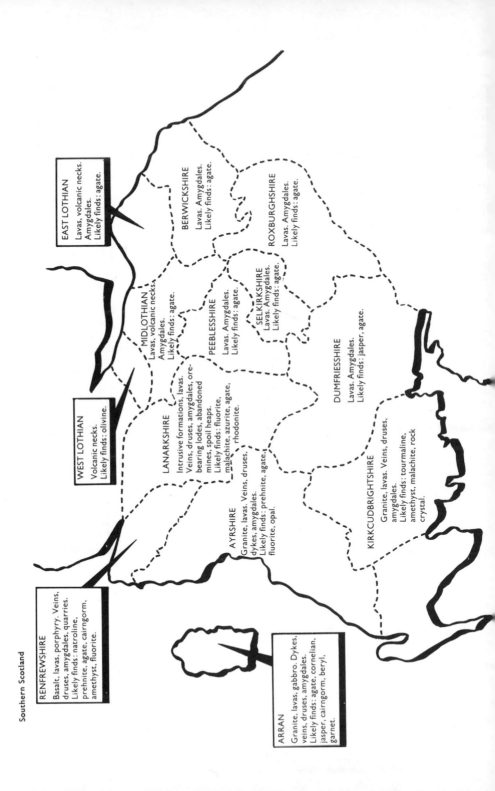

RENFREWSHIRE
Basalt, lavas, porphyry. Veins, druses, amygdales, quarries. Likely finds: natroline, prehnite, agate, cairngorm, amethyst, fluorite.

WEST LOTHIAN
Volcanic necks.
Likely finds: olivine.

EAST LOTHIAN
Lavas, volcanic necks. Amygdales.
Likely finds: agate.

MIDLOTHIAN
Lavas, volcanic necks, Amygdales.
Likely finds: agate.

BERWICKSHIRE
Lavas, Amygdales.
Likely finds: agate.

ROXBURGHSHIRE
Lavas, Amygdales.
Likely finds: agate.

PEEBLESSHIRE
Lavas, Amygdales.
Likely finds: agate.

SELKIRKSHIRE
Lavas, Amygdales.
Likely finds: agate.

LANARKSHIRE
Intrusive formations, lavas. Veins, druses, amygdales, ore-bearing lodes, abandoned mines, spoil heaps. Likely finds: fluorite, malachite, azurite, agate, rhodonite.

DUMFRIESSHIRE
Lavas, Amygdales.
Likely finds: jasper, agate.

AYRSHIRE
Granite, lavas. Veins, druses, dykes, amygdales. Likely finds: prehnite, agate, fluorite, opal.

KIRKCUDBRIGHTSHIRE
Granite, lavas, druses, amygdales. Likely finds: tourmaline, amethyst, malachite, rock crystal.

ARRAN
Granite, lavas, gabbro. Dykes, veins, druses, amygdales. Likely finds: agate, cornelian, jasper, cairngorm, beryl, garnet.

Central Scotland

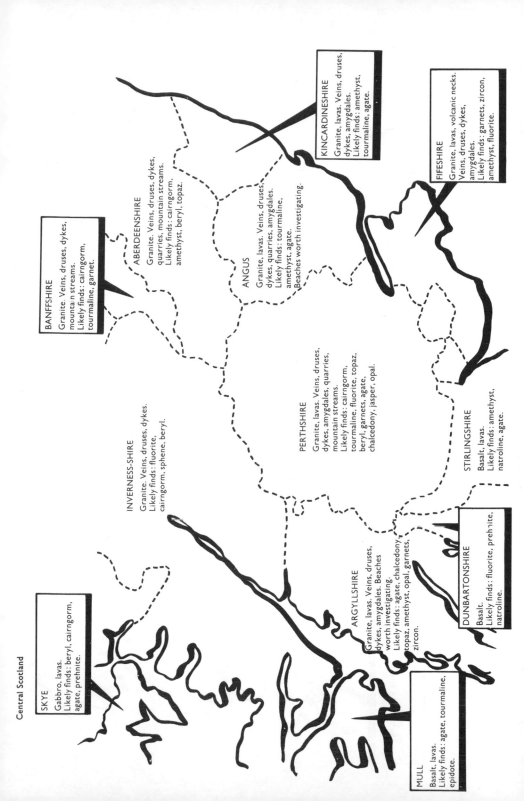

SKYE
Gabbro, lavas.
Likely finds: beryl, cairngorm,
agate, prehnite.

BANFFSHIRE
Granite. Veins, druses, dykes,
mounta n streams.
Likely finds: cairngorm,
tourmaline, garnet.

INVERNESS-SHIRE
Granite. Veins, druses, dykes.
Likely finds: fluorite,
cairngorm, sphene, beryl.

ABERDEENSHIRE
Granite. Veins, druses, dykes,
quarries, mountain streams.
Likely finds: cairngorm,
amethyst, beryl, topaz.

KINCARDINESHIRE
Granite, lavas. Veins, druses,
dykes, amygdales.
Likely finds: amethyst,
tourmaline, agate.

ANGUS
Granite, lavas. Veins, druses,
dykes, quarries, amygdales.
Likely finds: tourmaline,
amethyst, agate.
Beaches worth investigating.

FIFESHIRE
Granite, lavas, volcanic necks.
Veins, druses, dykes,
amygdales.
Likely finds: garnets, zircon,
amethyst, fluorite.

PERTHSHIRE
Granite, lavas. Veins, druses,
dykes, amygdales, quarries,
mountain streams.
Likely finds: cairngorm,
tourmaline, fluorite, topaz,
beryl, garnets, agate,
chalcedony, jasper, opal.

STIRLINGSHIRE
Basalt, lavas.
Likely finds: amethyst,
natroline, agate.

ARGYLLSHIRE
Granite, lavas. Veins, druses,
dykes, amygdales. Beaches
worth investigating.
Likely finds: agate, chalcedony,
topaz, amethyst, opal, garnets,
zircon.

DUNBARTONSHIRE
Basalt.
Likely finds: fluorite, prehite,
natroline.

MULL
Basalt, lavas.
Likely finds: agate, tourmaline,
epidote.

Northern Scotland

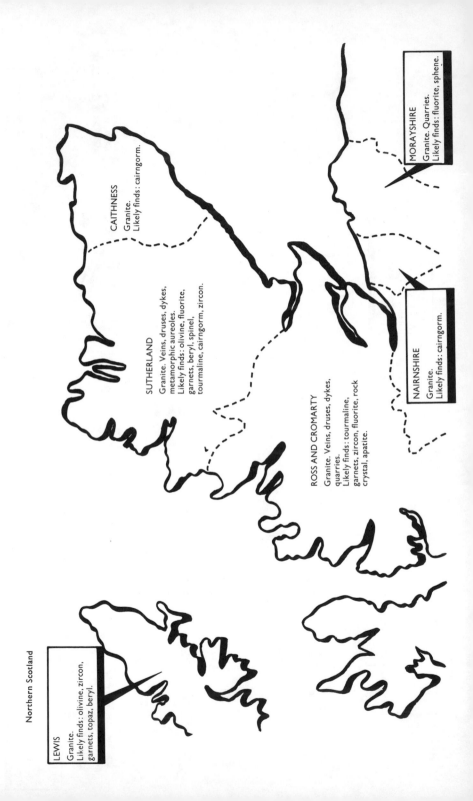

CAITHNESS

Granite.
Likely finds: cairngorm.

SUTHERLAND

Granite. Veins, druses, dykes,
metamorphic aureoles.
Likely finds: olivine, fluorite,
garnets, beryl, spinel,
tourmaline, cairngorm, zircon.

ROSS AND CROMARTY

Granite. Veins, druses, dykes,
quarries.
Likely finds: tourmaline,
garnets, zircon, fluorite, rock
crystal, apatite.

MORAYSHIRE

Granite. Quarries.
Likely finds: fluorite, sphene.

NAIRNSHIRE

Granite.
Likely finds: cairngorm.

LEWIS

Granite.
Likely finds: olivine, zircon,
garnets, topaz, beryl.

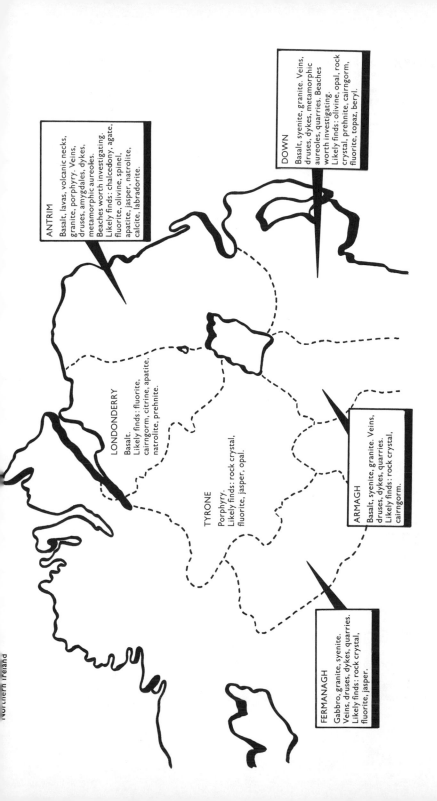

Northern Ireland

ANTRIM

Basalt, lavas, volcanic necks, granite, porphyry. Veins, druses, amygdales, dykes, metamorphic aureoles. Beaches worth investigating. Likely finds: chalcedony, agate, fluorite, olivine, spinel, apatite, jasper, natrolite, calcite, labradorite.

DOWN

Basalt, syenite, granite. Veins, druses, dykes, metamorphic aureoles, quarries. Beaches worth investigating. Likely finds: olivine, opal, rock crystal, prehnite, cairngorm, fluorite, topaz, beryl.

LONDONDERRY

Basalt. Likely finds: fluorite, cairngorm, citrine, apatite, natrolite, prehnite.

TYRONE

Porphyry. Likely finds: rock crystal, fluorite, jasper, opal.

ARMAGH

Basalt, syenite, granite. Veins, druses, dykes, quarries. Likely finds: rock crystal, cairngorm.

FERMANAGH

Gabbro, granite, syenite. Veins, druses, dykes, quarries. Likely finds: rock crystal, fluorite, jasper.

Index
The figures in bold refer to the colour illustrations between pp. 60 and 61 and 76 and 77.